Security in the Digital World

For the home user, parent, consumer and home office

Security in the Digital World

For the home user, parent, consumer and home office

GRAHAM DAY

IT Governance Publishing

Every possible effort has been made to ensure that the information contained in this book is accurate at the time of going to press, and the publisher and the author cannot accept responsibility for any errors or omissions, however caused. Any opinions expressed in this book are those of the author, not the publisher. Websites identified are for reference only, not endorsement, and any website visits are at the reader's own risk. No responsibility for loss or damage occasioned to any person acting, or refraining from action, as a result of the material in this publication can be accepted by the publisher or the author.

Apart from any fair dealing for the purposes of research or private study, or criticism or review, as permitted under the Copyright, Designs and Patents Act 1988, this publication may only be reproduced, stored or transmitted, in any form, or by any means, with the prior permission in writing of the publisher or, in the case of reprographic reproduction, in accordance with the terms of licences issued by the Copyright Licensing Agency. Enquiries concerning reproduction outside those terms should be sent to the publisher at the following address:

IT Governance Publishing
IT Governance Limited
Unit 3, Clive Court
Bartholomew's Walk
Cambridgeshire Business Park
Ely, Cambridgeshire
CB7 4EA
United Kingdom
www.itgovernance.co.uk

First published in the United Kingdom in 2017
by IT Governance Publishing.

ISBN 978-1-84928-961-0

DEDICATION

Sincerest acknowledgement to my wife Brenda - my chief
researcher - without whom this 'home project' would never
have been released with the hope of informing and enabling
others to be information security aware in this digital age.

PREFACE

The Internet and digital technology are the future; they are invaluable resources to be grasped and explored by all. The aim of this book is to empower people to surf safer online and manage their digital presence by being aware of how they might be attacked, how attackers may try to manipulate them or how their information might be at risk.

ACKNOWLEDGEMENTS

I would like to thank Chris Evans, Christopher Wright, Giuseppe G. Zorzino and Maarten Souw for their helpful comments during the review process.

ABOUT THE AUTHOR

Graham Day spent 24 years in the military, including more than a decade as a counter intelligence and security specialist on operational deployments around the globe.

Since retiring from the military, Graham has provided a range of services as a consultant, including, but not limited to, information security, cyber security, business continuity, cyber risk and cyber resilience.

He is currently working as a senior standards analyst for Equinix Ireland, responsible for compliance and instigation of best practice in security, business continuity, data protection and quality management.

Graham is a CESG Certified Professional Security Information Risk Advisor, a Certified Information Systems Security Professional and a member of the Author Group for British Standard 31111 Cyber Risk & Resilience.

CONTENTS

INTRODUCTION

When you lock your home at night you feel secure, confident that no attacker can get into your home without being detected. When you connect to the Internet that changes, you are creating a path for attackers to get into your home, your safe place, your sanctuary.

This book started as a project to help family and friends navigate the Internet safely and have some control of their digital presence. As an information and cyber security professional I continually support international companies in preventing attacks and managing incidents, but I am also very conscious that there is no single resource for the public.

As my personal project developed it was suggested there was too much helpful guidance and advice to not share outside the family. It is my hope that this book helps everyone prevent an attack or manage their online presence; if it does that for just one person then I will be very happy.

It is not my mission to change the world, but I would like to empower everybody to understand the threats and develop the culture to manage their digital presence.

The main caveat is that the information in this book is as good as the day it is written. Since that day there will have been new attacks and also possibly some changes to the actions you need to perform on your devices to be safer online.

Technology and threats are ever-evolving, use the information in this book as a baseline, then stay on top of updates, patches and safety settings to manage the risk of becoming a victim of an attack, or having your information used against you.

This book does not suggest companies are irresponsible, failing to protect their customers, or keeping their customers oblivious to the risks and threats to technologies, such as contactless cards. As a user I see various notices and warnings that businesses provide, but I am conscious that there is no single resource that explains how, why and what to do about them, which is what I have tried to create.

There are three things an attack needs: a means, a method and a motive. The means is the Internet or your device, the method is generally social engineering or malware, and the motive is your personal, financial or even work information.

I will go through who may be launching these attacks, as well as why, where and how.

I will also cover some things you can do to your device, the way you do things online, how you use technology and how you conduct yourself – all to protect yourself.

Unless you want to lock yourself away from society at large there is no gold-plated solution to staying safe, but lots of little things will combine into a better security posture and approach, a security blanket in effect that will cover you and give you some protection, that will hopefully help you be more aware and stay safe.

Safe surfing!

PERSONAL DIGITAL SECURITY TOP TEN

The juicy stuff first: here are the top ten things that can be done to put some personal or home cyber security in place. Some of these may already have been done, but there's no harm in being reminded. These are not in any specific order, but together they will give you a secure foundation;

1. *Configure the 'platform' – or 'secure your device'*

   Apply security settings in device config (see section 4.1)

   Install anti-malware applications (see Chapter 4)

   Schedule updates and patches (see section 5.1)

2. *Manage your accounts*

   Use passphrases or difficult passwords (see section 5.1)

   Use different security info for different accounts (see section 5.1) and multi-factor authentication whenever it is available (see section 5.1)

   Do not share your security info (see section 5.1)

3. *Have a private life*

   Do not post your personal or private information online (see section 3.1)

Do not post plans online, these could reveal a time when your home or you could be attacked (see section 3.1)

Do not be afraid to ask friends to take down posts about you, or that you are tagged in (see section 3.1)

4. Be security aware

Check the identification of senders of information, requests and callers (see section 3.1)

Challenge requests of callers if you have any doubts (see section 3.1)

Confirm the request is genuine with the company or organisation (see section 3.1)

5. Manage your information

Only entrust your information with providers you trust (see Chapter 8)

Regularly check your credit rating (see section 3.2)

Regularly search your own name online, as well as the names of your family (see section 3.2)

6. Build a secure web browser – configure your browser

Configure spam and ad blockers (see section 1.8)

Install an Internet security application (see Chapter 1)

Install a virtual private network (VPN) for mobile security (see section 6.3)

7. *Manage the home network and Internet of Things*

Change default passwords on devices (see section 10.1)

Configure network security applications (see section 5.1)

Regularly change the network passphrase (see section 5.1)

8. *Shop clever*

Check the security credentials of the site (see section 8.1)

Don't save credit/debit card details on websites (see section 8.2)

Use different browsers for different tasks (see section 1.4)

9. *Security does not stand still*

Regularly review your security (see section 3.2)
Take action if you notice anything different in your online presence or profile (see section 3.2)
Ask friends to inform you if they see anything online about you or that you need to know (see Chapter 11)

10. *Think twice, click once*

Do not commit to anything online until you have considered it and the impact on you (see section 12.1)

Do not take everything at face value as it only takes a minute to check (see section 12.1)

Once all points have been considered, reconsider before you act – think before you click! (see section 12.1)

Remember the 'five Ps': <u>Platform</u> (secure device), <u>Patches</u> (and updates), <u>Passwords,</u> <u>Privacy</u> and <u>Phishing.</u>

CHAPTER 1: THE INTERNET

When you use the Internet you are potentially creating a path for an attacker to get into your personal space, or to get your information. There are security controls you can put in place and also a few key behaviours for using the Internet that will better protect your information.

1.1 Connecting

The first thing to do for the internet is secure the connection. The ways to connect to the internet are introduced here as it is logical to understand this before you connect, but they are explained in greater detail in later sections.

Home networks (section 5.1) – this connection is secured by the home network encryption (section 5.1) and secured by password or passphrase (section 5.1).

Mobile network (section 6.3) – this connection is generally used when you are mobile. This connection should be secured with a VPN (section 6.3) if you are accessing important information or using your payment card.

Public wi-fi (section 6.2) – this connection should be used whenever you are in a public place and using provided wi-fi. For example, airports, trains, buses, coffee shops, restaurants, etc. This connection is secured through a VPN.

Note*. A VPN is a Virtual Private Network, it is a secure channel created between you and the target website.*

1.2 Browsers

There are a number of browsers available that you can use to search the Internet. Each browser has a different profile, how well it integrates with search engines, how fast it responds to requests, what features are built in, how fast it takes to reload, how quickly it downloads, etc. Below are some of the more popular free browsers.

Mozilla Firefox

Mozilla Firefox has been around for a number of years but has never been a front-runner. The issues with Microsoft Internet Explorer have, however, led to an increase in the use of Firefox as a default browser.

Mozilla Firefox can be customised to your requirements, is fast and secure, and protects your privacy.

Google Chrome

Google Chrome is inarguably the most widely used browser, with a 60% share of the market. It is unique in that it applies a single sign-on managing a number of Cloud-based personal applications, including Gmail (email), a calendar and personal notes. Google Chrome is also an advanced browser in the way security is applied, using two-factor authentication through a person's smartphone. Google Chrome is regularly updated.

Google Chrome is a fast browser but is not the quickest. It has strong security features and a very simple interface, and other features are available and easily installed.

Opera

This browser has a built-in VPN (see section 6.3 to understand the advantages of this), an ad blocker and a battery saver mode.

Microsoft Edge

This is the new browser from Microsoft that has been issued from Windows 10 onwards. It has a good interface, offers good security and supports extensions that can increase the number of functions.

Vivaldi

This browser is fully customisable, fast and 'fun' to use, although it lacks the features of other browsers.

Internet Explorer

This is probably the most widely known Internet browser, but some versions may cause unnecessary risk to home users. The latest versions of Internet Explorer – IE10 and IE11 – remain supported, but any new Windows operating systems will be released with Microsoft Edge, or any later browser Microsoft creates.

Supported or not supported – what does it mean?

If a browser is supported it means the developer will issue updates to fix vulnerabilities. If a browser is not supported, no updates will be issued. Whether a browser is supported is very important to the user's security.

☑ Regularly check the security of your browser. Make sure updates are applied.

☑ Look at the settings in your browser. If necessary, research the settings and apply them to make your browser as secure as possible.

1.3 Browser history

One thing you can do to protect yourself online, especially when you are using a public or shared computer, is to delete your browser history. There are two ways to do this:

Permanently – this is done in the 'Settings' or 'Options'. Within this menu there will be an option to 'Clear browsing data' when you close the browser. Within the 'Clear browsing data' menu there will also be options to clear cookies, cache and other groups such as download history and even stored passwords. All of these things should be selected for as far back as possible; some browsers may offer to do this for a certain period of time, be it hours, days or weeks, or 'from the beginning of time'.

Session, when closing the browser – as well as the permanent option in the browser 'Settings' or 'Option's menu, there will be a 'History' tab that will allow you to clear the session browsing history. This will only clear the browsing history and is not nearly as effective as the permanent option.

1. To clear your browsing history in Google Chrome go to the browser menu and select 'Settings' (3 vertical dots)

2. To clear history, go to 'Clear browsing data'

3. Make sure you select 'the beginning of time' for all options and click 'CLEAR BROWSING DATA' as shown above.

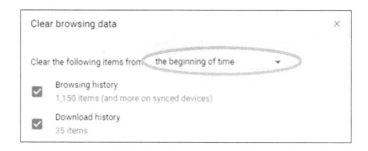

1.4 Tabs

Many browsers allow you to open multiple tabs in a session, but this can create a chance for an attacker to get sensitive information. If an attacker has got access to your internet session, then they could potentially access all tabs you have open (a session is from when you open the internet browser until you close it).

Social networking sites are a preferred way for attackers to get access to your online session. By not doing your online banking in the same session as having a social networking site open there is less possibility the online banking session will be compromised or breached.

There are a few things you can do to prevent this.

☑ Have a browser that you only use to access sites where sensitive information will be used.

☑ Have a different browser for searches and other general web access, such as Facebook.

☑ If you find an item to buy during a search, open the link to the chosen item in a new window to buy it, closing the first window before buying.

☒ Do not open sensitive sites in the same session as general access, such as searches or Facebook.

One thing you could do is have multiple browsers. For example, you could have three browsers available on your system:

1. One to access sensitive information, such as banks, medical, social, shopping, etc.
2. One to manage your professional profile, email, LinkedIn, etc.
3. One for general things such as searches and to access your social network, Facebook, etc.

1.5 Search engine

There are a number of search engines available, with five introduced below. These five are considered the primary search engines. Each of these search engines are free to use.

As a rule, search engines are financed by advertising. Search engines will return sponsored pages as the initial results of your search, then return the results that appear to be most closely associated with your search topic or feature keywords from your search. There are a number of risks with search engines, with the main one being that you trust the search engine to return genuine and safe results. The search engine's results are based on topic and/or keywords, so it is possible that the primary results are laden with malware or misinformation but have been built with keywords featured in common searches.

The main way to protect yourself from potentially malicious websites that exploit search engine algorithms is to be very conscious of the risk that many search terms will return results that may have malware in them, and if you go to the page there is a real risk that your system could be infected. People who want to implant this malware in your system or device will be very aware of the common search topics and will build sites that will be returned as results. They hope that you visit their site so they can infect your system or device, then their malware can change your system, give them access to your system or just bombard you with spam. When you view results, be very careful of the sponsored results that are usually very near the top and those that are not clearly related to your search term.

Another option is to use a search filter or McAfee WebAdvisor (section 1.6), and there are also add-ons for browsers such as Google and Firefox.

Google.com

Google has the largest catalogue of web pages available, and it is fast and relevant. Google also has excellent extra features to filter for images, news, maps and more.

Duckduckgo.com

Duckduckgo has some very good features, such as the 'zero click' information where all your responses are found on the first page. Duckduckgo is a clean, fast and efficient search engine that also offers prompts to help clarify the question you are asking and has less ad spam than most search engines.

Bing.com

Bing is regarded as the second most popular search engine. Until 2009, Bing was known as MSN Search. Bing tries to help you with your search by offering suggestions and gives you various search options.

Dogpile.com

Dogpile is a search engine with a quick, clean presentation, a growing index of web pages and helpful cross-link results.

Yippy.com

Yippy is a 'deep web' search engine: it searches other search engines. If you are searching for obscure material, Yippy is the best option.

1.6 McAfee WebAdvisor

McAfee WebAdvisor – previously SiteAdvisor – is an effective tool for protecting users from the 'dark' side of the Internet. WebAdvisor is a free to download and use Internet filter and protection application. There are four features in WebAdvisor that McAfee says on its website (*www.mcafee.com*) do the following:

1. Misclick protection – blocks phishing and malware sites if you click a link.

2. Typo protection – protects you if you incorrectly type a web address, and reportedly "points you in the right direction".
3. Safer downloads – scans your downloads and tells you if there is a "known risk".
4. Security check – checks your antivirus and firewall are turned on before you access the Internet.

1.7 Spam filter

A spam filter is an email feature that blocks unwanted spam emails from a user's inbox. Spam filters work by looking at the origin of an email, the signatures in the email and even the content. There are certain types of origin addresses associated with spam emails: this is the first filter. The second filter is the signatures: spam will have common types of signatures in their properties that the filter will identify and block. The third filter is the content: spam emails are created by applications that send emails to millions of addresses at the same time, and these applications use a common type of language that filters can recognise and block.

There is no guarantee that spam filters will be 100% effective but they will help you manage the types of emails that are received in your inbox. The ideal spam filter will be the filter designed to work with whichever email provider you are using, e.g. Gmail or Outlook.

1.8 Ad blocker

An ad blocker is a software tool that removes advertising content from a website, a web page or even a mobile app.

There are plenty of commercially available ad blockers, including an extension for Google Chrome, plus there are some available free from filehippo.com as discussed in section 4.2.

There is no guarantee that the ad blocker will be 100% effective, but it will block the majority of ads, and help you manage the information sent to your inbox, as well as ads which appear when you are surfing the Internet.

1.9 Cookies

Cookies are little bits of information that websites store on your computer about your visit to their website. For example, a grocery retailer will save cookies when you browse their store. The cookies will tell them what you looked at in the store, and even if there is a particular item that you looked at more than once. The cookies will also tell them if you revisit the store, and what you looked at during your next visit. The retailer will collect all this information and analyse it. If you have an account with the retailer, they will probably send you marketing or even offers for the items you looked at most often. The retailer is banking that if they can get you to do your shopping with them by giving you the targeted offers, based on the cookies collected from your previous visits, you will spend more money in the store than just for the offers.

The retailer will also be able to analyse the cookies from a greater number of people, which can be used to manage its stores and stocks more efficiently. For example, the retailer could work out what brand or type of products are likely to sell in certain areas or regions in comparison to other products. By working out this information, the retailer can order stock appropriately, but more importantly not order stock that is not going to sell in the area or region.

The retailer can even work out what women buy more than men, what men are looking for before Valentine's Day, and what products or types of product certain age groups will buy. Along with other information such as the number of men, women, students, married men, parents, etc., the retailer can manage all its stock ordering, offers and displays in certain areas or regions to maximise potential sales and reduce waste or effort.

Websites that collect cookies have to tell you that they are collecting these cookies and give you the option to agree to them doing so. You can refuse to accept the cookies policy, but this could result in you not being able to access a site that you may be registered with.

1.10 Email

There are a number of free email providers available for home users. Attackers may try to attack your email or even attack you by email. Here are five security tips:

1. Do not use an obvious username. Include numbers in your username, which makes it harder to guess as these could be random or only mean something to you.
2. Use a passphrase for your email that only you know and that you can remember.
3. If security questions are used to recover access then think about the security questions that would be used if you forget your passphrase. These security questions should be easy to answer for you but should

not be obvious answers, e.g. not your dog's name when this is posted on your social profile.

4. Have two-factor authentication if possible. Providers such as Google use this. Two-factor authentication for email uses something you know (your passphrase) and something you have (such as your phone) for you to access, which makes it harder for someone to hack into your account. As an example, if your phone is used as the second factor then a text message might be sent to your registered phone which contains a code, which you must enter into the application to access.

5. Do not save your username and password on computers or devices that you share, and do not share the passphrase to access your email.

Zoho Mail

Zoho Mail is a free service that has plenty of features, a thoughtfully designed interface and solid security. With the free account you get 5GB for mail and 5GB for documents. There is also a collection of web-based software to create documents and an integrated calendar.

Gmail

Gmail allows email to be easily imported from other accounts and contacts, so switching to the service is very easy. It automatically filters email into 'Primary', 'Social', 'Promotions' and 'Forums', it allows you to label messages instead of using folders, there are many ways to view emails, and overall it is an excellent service.

Outlook

Outlook is another excellent service that is comparable to Gmail. There are many very good features, such as the ability to archive emails, sort emails into folders, flag emails, and import contacts from Facebook and elsewhere.

1.11 iCloud

iCloud is a service associated with iPhones and iPads. iCloud is a simple email service that comes with 5GB of free iCloud storage. There are folders to organise emails, rules can be created to sort emails as they arrive in your inbox, it has an easy-to-use interface, and you can identify senders as a VIP so their emails always go into the VIP inbox and they will not be missed.

CHAPTER 2: THE THREATS

2.1 Cyber crime

Cyber crime is a criminal activity that involves a computer or digital media and a network – in most cases, the Internet.

Cyber crime allows anyone to become a criminal: a person who is technically inept, or who lacks the confidence to challenge another person, or lacks the guile of a fraudster or anyone who is not able to be a criminal in the traditional sense of the word. The computer gives them a shield to hide behind, and gives them the means to attack without being seen or heard, and without being near the victim or having any connection to the victim.

Attackers are slowly discovering all the ways that devices can be used to attack others. As this knowledge develops, the number and sophistication of attacks also increase.

2.2 The who?

There are two very different types of attackers who must be understood to help you protect yourself. There are the brazen, confident, imposing, threatening, violent and overt attackers, while the other attackers are deceptive, covert and manipulative. Attackers who intimidate, threaten violence, are violent or are extremely abusive are the former, and Internet attackers – manipulators, tricksters and fraudsters – are generally the latter. Internet attackers are also technologists, using technology and people's lack of understanding of technology to get what they want.

Hackers and crackers

There are two types of people who know computers, networks and programming: hackers and crackers. Hackers use their knowledge to find vulnerabilities or weaknesses in computer systems and then try to fix them. Hackers in the truest form are ethical hackers: they are available for hire to attack a computer system or network to test the security in place so that the organisation can improve it.

Crackers use their knowledge for their own benefit or gain. There has been much confusion about these terms, to the extent that 'hacker' is now used to describe both types of people without making any distinction as to whether or not the 'hacker' is using their skills and knowledge for good.

To avoid confusion, the generalised term 'hacker' is used in this book to refer to a person who uses their knowledge and experience to find vulnerabilities or weaknesses in a computer system, whether it is for ethical purposes or otherwise.

Hacking has become an industry in its own right, with hackers advertising their services and distributing their tools as products for sale. They tend to work alone but occasionally collaborate to achieve a common aim, either for a specific period of time or until the common goal has been achieved. From these collaborations groups may form that collectively are very resourceful and clever because they tend to share knowledge and experience, and have more time between them than a lone person.

Groups of computer hackers who use their skills and knowledge to further a political agenda or personal belief are called 'hacktivists'. 'State-sponsored' hackers are teams that have phenomenal computing resources, as well as the infrastructure and support to dedicate their whole time and effort to an aim.

Among all of these types of hackers are the script kiddies, who try to be hackers without the knowledge and experience. They will collect malware or code from the Internet, copy it or change it slightly, and launch it back onto the Internet. While they lack any real experience or understanding of the tools they use, script kiddies can still be quite destructive simply because they don't really understand what their tools may be capable of.

Traditionally, hackers have mainly targeted commercial organisations or governments, be it for monetary gain or commercial espionage, or to cause political upset or influence public opinion. However, hackers are now targeting home networks as much as commercial entities or public bodies. Home users are running their own networks, and some professionals are using their home networks to manage company information, but home networks are almost always less secure than corporate networks.

As well as the professional information that could be taken from a home network, there are other reasons these may be attacked. If there is a baby monitor, the images could be sold to child pornographers. There may be personal information that would enable an attacker to steal an identity or financial information, or access credentials that could provide access to financial accounts. With the Internet of Things (IoT), even more information can be gleaned from home networks, such as when the home is vacant, which could be passed on to burglars. A hacker might also try to insert malicious software (malware) onto home networks. Such malware will have a specific purpose, which I'll discuss later.

Internet trolls

Internet trolls are quite unique in their intent. They generally exist in social media and do not seek personal gain in a tangible form such as money, but instead seek satisfaction or even some form of revenge through seeing the distress caused to another person online. Internet trolls start arguments, quarrels or disagreements online in order to get their satisfaction. Internet trolls have been grouped according to their 'trait', their mannerism or even their characteristic. These groupings include:

Insult troll – will pick on anyone for no apparent reason and post insults to or about them.

Persistent debate troll – just live for a good argument.

Spelling and grammar troll – try to show how clever they are or even suggest a comparison with somebody. These trolls may not even be blatant in exhibiting their characteristic. They might make a spelling or grammar observation in a post, sometimes in inverted commas or quotes to highlight it.

Blabbermouth troll – not necessarily interested in contributing to a thread or topic. These trolls will post so that they can be seen and acknowledged, maybe even posting something that is irrelevant to the topic or thread but is all about themselves, usually suggesting how good they think they are.

Exaggeration trolls – will post any response to blow any topic out of proportion.

Other threats

There are lots of other threats that exist online which are discussed later in the book, in the section on parental security. A very brief introduction of some of these threats is below. Greater detail of each of these threats is included in the parent's section. The main source of information should be child protection agencies websites, such as NSPCC, ISPCC and/or American SPCC, who will have the greatest detail, current information and also advice, guidance and contacts of where help is available.

Cyber bullying

Cyber bullying is a means for anyone to be a bully as potentially there is no physical connection between the bully and the victim, it is all done by electronic means. Traditional bullies rely on physical presence or group pressure; cyber bullies can be without these aspects. Where a person who did not have the physical presence was not able to be a traditional bully, they can be a cyber bully.

Cyber bullying has two significant aspects that means it differs, and is significantly more of an issue, to traditional bullying;

It is relentless, a child retreating into their safe zone, their home or bedroom, is no longer guaranteed to escape the online bullying as the internet is invited into the home or safe space.

It is not restricted to a single method of bullying. Where traditional bullying is primarily experienced when the victim physically meets the bully cyber bullying can be experienced at any time, on any medium i.e. on the mobile phone, the laptop, the tablet, the home computer, etc.

Cyber bullying is addressed in greater detail in section 12.

Grooming

Grooming requires a concentrated effort on the part of the attacker. Grooming is achieved by manipulating the victim based on a secret trust relationship.

Grooming develops from a single action which is used by the attacker as the foundation of the trust relationship. The single action could be from taking a sweet from a stranger to getting in a car with a stranger, or any other number of actions which might be forbidden by the parent's but encouraged by the attacker. Once the single action has happened the attacker uses this to gradually increase the appearance of trust, for example the child talks to the stranger, then the child takes a sweet from the stranger, then gets in the car, etc. This trust escalation will continue until the attacker, the groomer, gets what they want from the child.

Grooming is spoken about in greater detail in the parent's section and there will be more detail on the websites of child protection agencies.

Sextortionists

Sextortionists have a different attack method to grooming attackers, although ultimately their intent might be the same. Sextortionists will base their attack on a single action of the victim that the sextortionist gets hold of, for example by cloning the victim's phone or hacking their picture or text storage, then exploits. The attacker will exploit this by telling the victim they will release the image, text or other incriminating or embarrassing media, unless the victim does something for the attacker.

2.3 The why

Internet attackers are generally after one of two things: either to better themselves by getting money or goods, or to prove to themselves how clever they are. The attackers who want to prove how clever they are tend to attack companies, organisations or government agencies. The attackers who want to get money tend to be the threat that home users and normal Internet users should be concerned about. The reason these attackers prey on normal Internet users is they feel the users are not trained, are not aware of the threats, and are gullible or can be manipulated.

There is another type of attacker who mainly targets children for sexual exploitation, which is mentioned in the parent's section. There are also many agencies that would be 'official' references and would have current reporting of these threats. These agencies would include such bodies as the NSPCC in UK, ISPCC in Ireland and American SPCC in the US. Each of these agencies, in addition to policing agencies, will have websites where further information can be found.

Financial gain

The primary motivation for the majority of attacks is financial, whether it is money the attacker can get directly from the attack or from another person who could benefit from the spoils of the attack. Attackers who launch a ransomware attack are looking for immediate financial gain, whereas another attacker might capture a victim's financial details to sell to another person, which would be an indirect gain.

Corporate information

Attackers who target corporate information are also looking for financial gain, either directly or indirectly. Attackers seeking direct gain could use the information gained to benefit from a merger or an acquisition that could only be discovered from a breach, whereas an attacker seeking indirect gain might take the information gained to plan a physical attack, even going so far as to kidnap or extort money from the company.

Home users may be attacked by 'professional' attackers who want to get corporate information. Although workers are often told not to use their home computers for work, the attackers know that the workers will because it is easier and less hassle than taking the company laptop out, or there could be a time restriction that means work has to be done on the home computer. Attackers will target home networks to see how much corporate information they can get, which they could then use against the company or in another type of attack.

As well as corporate information being on home systems, there are also home offices. Businesses need to start somewhere, with the starting point generally being the home. Also, in some households the management or administration of the home and the family is down to one person who uses their home device.

Ego

An attacker with an egotistical motive is not seeking financial gain but is seeking recognition, acknowledging that the attacker has the skills and knowledge to defeat the security. There are far fewer ego-motivated attacks reported in comparison with financial or politically motivated attacks.

A significant attack that appeared to be ego-motivated was the Sony pictures hack in 2014. There may have been another motive initially but as all the images and data was made available soon after the hack it would suggest it was an ego-motivated attack.

It is probable no ego-motivated attacks actually start as ego-motivated attacks but happen accidentally. This could occur for example when exploring the hack of one agency then discover a vulnerability to another agency which could lead to greater discoveries.

2.4 The where

The general answer for the where is the Internet, as an attacker needs a surreptitious way in and the Internet is a path you have willingly put in place.

Threats also exist in the digital environment as technology becomes more integrated in our way of life. Between the technology we bring into the home or wear on our person, or even in us, the way our information is shared with one another, companies and official bodies, and the way we use technology to exchange information or make transactions, there are many opportunities for attackers unless we manage how we use technology, our information and our digital presence.

Specifically stating where a threat may exist is impossible as the possibilities are endless. There are some places where it would be easier for an attacker, or where an attacker has a proven, successful method. These prime locations include public Wi-Fi zones, ATMs (not in branch or store), shops using contactless payments, shops using chip and PIN, and enclosed areas of congregation.

CHAPTER 3: THE HOW

There are a number of attacks that aim to manipulate you into giving an attacker your money or personal information.

- 'Scareware', which scares you into doing something that will allow an attacker into your system or give your information to them.
- Ransoming your information, telling you that a ransom must be paid before you regain access to it.
- Diverting you to a false page where you may surrender your information.
- Getting you to reveal some of your secret information that you use to access accounts, such as usernames, passwords, or even a secret PIN or preferred security question.
- Getting you to reveal bank or credit card information.
- Getting you to reveal personal information, which could then be used to get money through identity theft.

Some attacks, meanwhile are not computer-based.

- Taking money off your cards.
- Making you give information over the telephone or in conversations.

- Persuading you to let them into your home or office where they can get information or even remove your valuable items.
- Getting your card information at cash machines or other payment points such as the ones in shops.
- Getting your information through a text message.

These methods may be used on their own or together. Attacks using more than one method are more difficult for the attacker to control but they do tend to have a greater chance of being successful. There is no rule as to how attacks might appear, but the people who put them together are extremely imaginative and will go to great lengths if they think they can profit.

These combined attacks could be any combination of email, text, telephone or even in-game chats. By using more than one type of communication, the attacker makes you more confident that you are not being duped or manipulated.

There are also technical threats, which are in the first instance delivered using some sort of social engineering.

Also the very fact a user is following a trend could be used against them, maybe to embarrass them or could even be used to determine suitability for a job. Imagine a person is posting comments opposing water charges in Ireland, or protesting Brexit in the UK, well these comments could be seen as opposing government, also known as seditious activity.

If an employer happened to conduct social profile analysis as an element of the recruitment process and they saw this seditious activity they might decide not to employ the individual. Alternatively, it might be known that Person A is applying for a role with a specific company, if the company does not do social profile analysis but is informed of the seditious activity by an attacker or another person with malicious intent that could impact the possibility of the Person A getting the job.

In this case the threat is the user themselves, not thinking about the possible damage or impact from their own posts!

3.1 Social engineering

What is it?

Social engineering is when an attacker tries to manipulate you into giving them either your information, or access to your computer so that they can get the information themselves. Social engineering can take place over many types of communication, from the person knocking at your door or ringing you on the telephone to emails, text messages, or chats within games or apps.

The range of social engineering attacks is ever-increasing: begging in the street for money with a baby to encourage people to give more, pretending to be an official to gain entry into a person's home, pretending to be a police officer conducting door-to-door enquiries looking for forged money, then running off with the victim's money, wallet and all their personal information – attackers are continually developing schemes.

Depending on the origin of the attack, it may be very difficult to detect a social engineering attack. Social engineering has been highly lucrative against certain types or groups of people, primarily those from an era where trust existed, those who have not really been exposed to the malicious nature of others, those who feel they are in dire need of escape from their current situation or those who may have learning difficulties.

For an attacker, social engineering is the preferred form of attack as the victim is tricked into revealing their information or letting the attacker into their home; there is no violence and the primary defence in court could be that the victim gave it to them or let them in.

Alternatively, the attacker will seek to capture enough information that they could use against the victim or even to plan a different type of attack against the victim.

The attacker may try to get future timings or plans so they know when to attack your home with minimal risk, especially if it has recently been posted online that you have a new prized possession or there has been a birthday or celebration in the home. Any one of these events could mean that there are attractive items in the home that the attacker is attracted to.

In every circumstance it is prudent to be very careful as a to what information you post, or is posted about you, online. If necessary, ask friends or family to remove posts.

Ultimately, the aim of social engineering is to exploit human nature by targeting common human traits: fear (that you could be attacked) and desire for betterment (to better your life through financial gain or improving your status).

What could be the impact – what does it mean to you?

An attacker's intent very much determines the impact on the victim. If the attacker gets access to someone's personal system, the attacker could get financial information that can be used to steal money, or personal details that can be used to steal someone's identity or even get credit in the victim's name.

The severity of the impact is determined by how much access to your information an attacker can get, whether that is by attacking your personal system or device, or by gathering lots of snippets of information that could then be brought together to build a fraudulent profile. The attacker is not concerned about the impact on you, only with how much they can gain from the attack.

There are lots of ways an attack could affect you:

Financial loss – this is the obvious one, as the majority of attacks are for financial gain.

Identity theft – this has the biggest potential impact because of the knock-on effects of being a victim of identity theft. Victims of identity theft could also suffer financial loss – in 2017 it was reported by the US news channel CNBC that the average financial loss to identity theft per person was over US$1,000 (*www.cnbc.com/2017/02/01/consumers-lost-more-than-16b-to-fraud-and-identity-theft-last-year.html*).

Attackers consistently increase in sophistication, enabling them to target more and more people, and potentially increasing the impact of their crimes.

Credit rating – this may not seem a big issue but it could prevent a person getting a mortgage or buying a car.

Criminal record – a stolen identity could be used for any number of nefarious activities, with the most basic being ordering items online but not paying for them, and the most extreme being terrorism. The range of penalties differ for these activities, from a short conversation with the authorities, to being blacklisted from visiting certain countries, to being detained when entering certain countries.

Emotional impact – some victims of identity theft have likened it to being raped or violated. There is no means to measure how much this will impact an individual, or even how long this feeling would last. Some people have reportedly disconnected from the Internet permanently after being the victim of identity theft.

Reputational damage – it can take a considerable amount of time to recover damage to your reputation following an attack, especially if the attacker actually intended to cause reputational damage. If it was the intent, the attacker would impersonate you online to have the greatest impact on you.

Recovery cost – as well as the actual cost of any losses, there are costs to recover from identity theft. These include legal fees, insurance, bank charges, and consultants' fees to help recover your credit rating.

Commercial loss – probably the easiest example of an attack causing commercial loss is CEO fraud: if an attacker is able to get information that would allow them to impersonate the CEO of an organisation then they could do any number of things with that authority before the identity theft was discovered. The worst-case scenario is an attacker falsely assuming the identity of the CEO and issuing directives, which could have very serious ramifications for the company.

An extra concern for victims of social engineering is the recovery of the loss, e.g. money, where banks or even cyber insurance may not refund the loss as it was willingly given by the victim, even though it was given based on a lie or being manipulated.

Social engineering attackers bank on their victim's ego. A victim may not report the attack, or even acknowledge being a victim, as they would not like to admit they have been manipulated. The best platform to admit to others of an attack is through social media – using the 'threat platform' against the attackers – to prevent other people being victims and reduce the chance of the attacker being successful.

Phishing

Phishing is social engineering by email. The email will tell you something and direct you to click a link that will take you to another page that the attacker has built. This page will ask you for information. The information that you enter in the second page will go straight to the attacker, who will use it to make money at your expense.

Here are some examples of phishing emails.

3: The how

Example 1: This looks like a genuine notification email from PayPal.

We have updates on our Policy Update page.

De

As you know, your transaction was recently declined. Let us explain so we can make sure it doesn't happen again. For your safety, we limit the amount of money that goes through your account. We do this to protect you, and us, from the rare occasions of fraud. Log in to my PayPal account and you can resolve your limitation by following all simple steps

As always, if you need help or have any questions, feel free to contact us. We're always here to help

Thank you for being a PayPal customer

Yours sincerely,
PayPal

Here are the key elements of this email.

P PayPal

We have updates on our Policy
Update page.

② Dear ▮▮▮@hotmail.com

As you know, your transaction was recently declined. Let us explain so we can make sure it doesn't happen again. For your safety, we limit the amount of money that goes through your account. We do this to protect you and us, from the rare occasions of fraud. Log in to ③ PayPal account and you can resolve your limitation by following all simple steps.

As always, if you need help or have any questions, feel free to contact us. We're always here to help.

Thank you for being a PayPal customer.

Yours sincerely,
PayPal

1. This message is put here to reassure you that this is a genuine email, and also to prompt you into doing something.

2. The message will be sent to your correct email address, which would have been pawned. See section 3.2 for more information on being pawned.

3. This is the link that the attacker wants you to click. It will take you to a page that looks the same as the PayPal login page but if you check the page in the address bar it would be different from the actual PayPal login page.

If the 'Log in to my PayPal account' link had been clicked, it would have taken you to the page *https://solver-authorizedpayment.com/*, which would look like the PayPal login page. If you had logged in to your account on that page, you would have given the attacker your username and password to access your PayPal account, from where they could transfer all of the money you had in there.

Does this look like a genuine PayPal email address?

What should you do?

- ☑ Check the sender's email address.
- ☑ Ask yourself if you have made a transaction on PayPal recently. If you didn't, be very suspicious. The first indicator that this email is not genuine is if you do not have a PayPal account in the first place.
- ☑ Don't click on any links in the email. Instead, hover your cursor over them to reveal the URL they will direct you to. The genuine PayPal login page is accessed from *www.paypal.com*. The address for the

login page will be an extension of this, such as *www.paypal.com/signin?country.x=IE&local.x=en_I E* (when accessing the sign-in page from Ireland (IE)). *https://solver-authorizedpayment.com/* which you will see when you hover over the link, does not look anything like the genuine *www.paypal.com/signin?country.x=IE&local.x=en_I E*. Be sure to check the link displayed carefully. They are designed to look as accurate as possible, such as paypa1.com, pay.pal.com, etc.

☑ When you are happy this is a phishing email, move the message to your junk or spam folder in your email account. Any other messages from this sender will go straight to your junk or spam folder in future.

Example 2: Annual tax refund – does the taxman routinely tell you he owes you money?

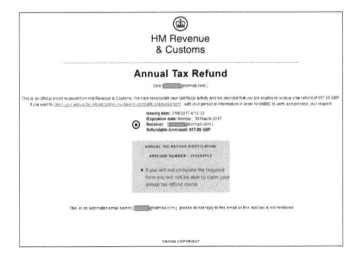

The content of this email is riddled with errors and mistakes that make it apparent it is a phishing email. Some are highlighted in the image below.

1. "We have recalculate" – is past tense so it should be 'We have recalculated'.
2. 657.99 GBP – the UK taxman would probably use £ instead of GBP.
3. 3/10/2017 – the UK taxman would not use the US date system.
4. "Ammount" – an obvious spelling error.
5. "If you will not complete" – this would not be correct in general conversation. It should be 'If you do not complete'.

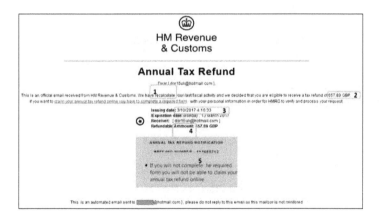

And then there is the sender's email address:

Does *bvljwm@chalmers.se* look like it is associated with the genuine HMRC website that will be from the *https://www.gov.uk* domain? The HMRC login page is at *https://www.gov.uk/log-in-register-hmrc-online-services* – does the origin email address resemble this in any way?

Not all phishing emails will be as riddled with errors as the second example, so the only way to stop yourself being caught out is by being diligent and really looking at an email before you commit to doing anything the email asks.

When phishing emails were first seen about fifteen years ago, they would talk about extravagant numbers and invite you to a scheme where you would have to make a payment to show how committed you were or to validate your bank account. Phishing emails today generally use more realistic amounts that are more likely to be accepted as real.

An attacker may also try to get you to trust their email by sending it from a friend's or other contact's account. This person may not even know their account has been breached.

Phishing emails are generally sent to email addresses that have been 'pwned'. It is quite probable that a phishing email will be from the same country as that of the company where the email was pawned. This will be apparent in the sender address of the phishing email. For example, if the company that was breached is registered in Ireland it is highly probable that the sender email is from an address with the country domain .ie. Cyber threats are geocentric, certain types of cyber threats will be used in certain countries, possibly where the attacker thinks the population are more likely to fall victim to the attack.

Another type of phishing email is the offer to check whether your credit card details are secure or have been compromised. The email will ask for all your credit card information, but you would in fact be giving your card details to an attacker. There is no official safe way to check whether your card details have been compromised.

What should you do?

There are a number of things that will help you identify phishing emails and stop you being caught out:

☑ Do you have an account with the 'sender' or do you recognise them?

☑ Type the actual site address in the address bar to go to the official site, and log in through the official site to see if any transactions have been completed on your account. Also see if there was a communication within your account, as many organisations have a communication function within the account for customer services.

☑ Is the origin email address genuine, does it link to the sending organisation and do you recognise it?

☑ Is the reference correct?

☑ Is the subject matter correct, e.g. have you recently made a transaction using that account?

☑ Is the grammar and spelling correct? Is the registered address correct in the email?

☑ Does it direct you to click a link? This should raise suspicion. **Never click a link in an email that you were not expecting or that you are suspicious of.**

☑ Put phishing emails into trash and create a rule if prompted.

Vishing

Vishing is social engineering using voice, such as a telephone call.

The main aim of vishing is to get your information, whether that is your personal information that an attacker can base an attack on, or your security information that could be used to further an attack.

If the aim is to get your personal information, the conversation may open with some generic statement regarding a topical issue that may be common among home users or personal users. An example of this exchange may be:

Caller: *Good day, I believe you may have an issue with your personal computing device.*

User: *I have, when I play movies the film pauses and sometimes stops.*

Caller: *That is an issue that I think I can help you with. Can I confirm your name, email address, mobile number and home Internet provider?*

User: *Certainly, it is….*

Caller: *That is fine, we can help you fix this. Can you also confirm who you bank with?*

User: *Okay, can I ask why you need that?*

Caller: *We have an agreement with certain banks that we can offer a reduced fee that is paid by the bank, so if you use one of those banks then we can help you free of charge.*

User: *That is excellent, I bank with….*

Caller: *Perfect! We have that agreement with them. If you can just give me your account number, then I can bill them directly and you will receive this support free.*

User: *It is….*

From this call, with very little or even no information to start with, the person doing the vishing has got the user's name, mobile number, email address, bank name, account number and Internet provider.

The person doing the vishing will possibly give some generic advice, such as recommending you do not use any other devices when you are watching a film to improve the viewing experience, or they may even state they have to get advice from a senior technician and ask you to confirm when you will next be home for them to call.

If you then said that you were out tomorrow all day at work but home in the evening, you have also told them your house will be empty for the next working day.

The other aim of vishing calls might be to get some of your secret information. Following the first call, a few days later you might receive a call like the following:

Caller: *Good day, Mr .... I am from your high street bank. We would like to offer you the opportunity to increase the security on your account. Please confirm you have this type of account and your account number, which I have as....*

User: *Oh, excellent. I am very conscious of security. That is my account number.*

Caller: *We are very happy to help, but I just need to go through some security checks with you. Your email address is ... and your mobile phone number is....*

User: *That is correct.*

Caller: *Excellent. Last thing: if you can just confirm the second and sixth digits of your PIN?*

User: *... and ....*

Caller: *I'm sorry, maybe I misheard you but that is not going through on my system. Perhaps if you can give me the first and fourth digits?*

User: *... and ....*

Caller: *Okay, that is allowing me to access. So, what we would like to do is direct you to an application that will allow you to access your account securely using public Wi-Fi networks, for example at the local coffee shop. The* *software creates a VPN, and you can download it from this website....*

From this call the person now has the first, second, fourth and sixth digits of your PIN to access the account for which they previously got the username information.

How many guesses would it take for them to work out the other two figures? Once they have your PIN they have complete access to your account.

There are many more ways that vishing can be used but generally there will be a trend: the caller will try to be your friend, they will try to establish a relationship by using first names or telling you they have the same problem, they will also try to further create the trust relationship between you. As the trust relationship develops you will tend to give more information, which is what the caller is banking on and will encourage you or guide this.

Vishing tends to be used with another method for getting your information directly, using your information against you or getting access to your information.

An example of this would be when someone is providing computer support and says that the issue is very difficult, and that they need to access your computer to fix it. They could state they have sent you an email with a link that you should click. Computer repair or security is a popular topic to manipulate you with because these are topics that most people choose not to understand or don't have the time to.

If you challenge the caller, they will probably state that if you don't give them the information then the service they are offering will cost you, or you might not even get the service. They will tell you whatever they think they need to so that you give them your information.

What can you do?

- ☒ Do not give personal or secret information to unknown callers.
- ☑ If the caller says they are from an official organisation, a bank or another institution that manages your sensitive information, such as a hospital, say you will call or visit your regular branch to provide the information instead of giving it over the telephone.
- ☒ Do not let yourself be manipulated into providing information despite what they may threaten.
- ☑ State that it is not a convenient time for you to speak and request a telephone number that you can call them back on. Also, get a reference number, the name of the person calling and the name of the organisation they represent.
- ☑ Use a different contact method to confirm whether the call is authentic. If you were approached by email then telephone the organisation. If you were approached by telephone then email customer service. At the very least, get the official contact number for the organisation from its website and dial that number. Do not use a number that was provided in the approach.
- ☑ Terminate the call.

Smishing

Smishing is social engineering using SMS (text messages). Text messages tend to be used with another method rather than by themselves. Smishing can be used to send attachments or links, which when clicked or opened take you to a vulnerable or false website, or install malware on your device that could allow an attacker to get your information.

A common smishing attack is a text that claims to be from your bank. Within the text there is a link that takes you to a site that is supposed to be your bank but is a false site. The false site is trying to get you to enter your information.

Smishing could also come from one of your 'contacts' whose phone has been copied or breached. Your contact may not even know their device has been copied or breached.

What can you do?

- ☒ Don't click links in text messages unless you know who the sender is.
- ☒ Don't click links unless the message is something you are expecting or it would be normal to receive this type of message from the sender.
- ☒ Don't open attachments unless you know the sender and are expecting the attachment.

- ☑ Call the sender to check they sent you the message and that the link in the message is safe.

Cat-phishing

Cat-phishing refers to false profiles on dating sites. Well-known dating sites include Tinder, Plenty of Fish and, more notoriously, Ashley Madison, which suffered a data breach in 2015. Some of these sites are discussed in the social networking security section.

Scareware

Scareware seeks to exploit our fears, to scare the person receiving it into doing something. Scareware attacks can be launched by email, telephone, the Internet or a combination of these.

There are many variations of scareware, all aiming to get the person receiving the email to do something, such as click something or pay for something that they do not actually need, or even install an application that they do not need.

Below is a scareware email. This email states that the person's account is being accessed from another device, which is intended to scare the person receiving the email into clicking the link to investigate. This is one type of scareware.

It is possible to see the embedded URL by hovering the cursor over the link. The link can be extremely long, as seen in the following image, or very short by using a link shortener such as Bit.ly (*https://techcrunch.com/2009/11/30/bit-ly-spam/*).

The email is telling the recipient that their account has been
accessed by a new device and a link is provided for the
recipient to "Update My Account".

If the provided link is clicked, the recipient will be taken to another site that will collect information entered, which could then be used for financial gain.

As well as monetary loss, the recipient will likely see their credit rating suffer.

3.2 Malware

Malware is malicious software that will damage or harm your computer, network or information. Malware comes in many forms, but the sole intent is to infect your system. Some malware will go on to attempt to take control of your system, allowing the attacker to do anything they want with it or the information on the device, deny you the device or the information, or benefit from taking control of the device or the information.

Technical threats

Every day malware is altered slightly by an attacker to create a new strain that does something different from the original. It is impossible to keep track of all the different strains, but the following terms will cover the majority.

Ransomware

Ransomware started off exclusively targeting organisations, but now home users can be just as much of a target. Ransomware takes control of the information on the system, encrypts it so that it cannot be read and then charges a ransom before unencrypting the information and making it readable again. Like other malware, ransomware evolves rapidly, and the latest types now take control of the system and prevent any kind of access unless the ransom is paid.

Ransomware-as-a-service is essentially ransomware for hire and is available on the dark web, which is an area of the Internet used for nefarious activities.

Two ransomware attacks were highly publicised in 2017: WannaCry hit the NHS in the UK, disrupting medical services, and NotPetya hit Ukraine, affecting its industries as well as some global companies, such as Maersk.

Zero day

A zero-day vulnerability is a term used to describe a vulnerability that has been identified before the manufacturer has realised and issued a fix in an update. The success of enthusiasts in discovering zero-day vulnerabilities has led to manufacturers offering rewards, known as 'bug bounties', if they are informed of zero days. Some enthusiasts have been so successful at identifying zero days that they do it professionally.

Jailbreak

Jailbreaking is a term used to describe the potential severity of an attack. This type of attack makes the device vulnerable at the very root. A successful jailbreak attack gives the attacker complete control of the device, allowing them to do with it whatever they want.

Trojan

A trojan is malware disguised as something else. It describes the delivery mechanism rather than the malware itself, so any kind of malware could be delivered via a trojan.

Worm

A worm is a type of malware that copies itself and moves to other computers, damaging those computers or the data on them. The original worm stays on the computer and continues to replicate itself, and each replicated version moves on to the next computer. Worms generally move over networked computers, using the network to move between the computers.

Worms carry code designed to modify the code on the infected computer in some way so that the computer does something different. The new code does what the author of the worm wants it to do, not what it was originally designed to do.

Virus

A virus is a type of malware that is moved between computers in an infected host file, such as an email attachment. The virus will damage the computer it infects or the information on it.

A virus is a program that will cause your system to do something you do not want it to do, but what an attacker wants it to do.

Bots

A bot is a computer that connects to a central computer system that acts as a command and control centre. The command and control system can use lots of bots at the same time to cause a problem for a particular company's website, such as flooding it with requests. Here, the bot is part of a larger group, a botnet, that is used in what is called a distributed denial-of-service attack (DDoS).

A botnet is not an attack on your system but is actually using the system to take part in a DDoS. A personal computer or device can be part of a botnet without the user knowing it.

Any device that connects to the Internet has the ability to be part of a botnet. Recent DDoS attacks have used devices like digital cameras to launch the attack, so all the digital cameras were part of the botnet. Another recent DDoS attack was launched using IP-based cameras, which are generally used as 'nanny-cams' or as domestic internal CCTV.

Exploit

The Oxford English Dictionary definition of the word exploit is: make full use of and derive benefit from (a resource) or make use of (a situation) in a way considered unfair or underhand!

In cyber security the term exploit is used to define a malware code that can be used against a system, generally if there is a known vulnerability or even a 'zero day'. The exploit is built to expose the vulnerability.

In information security the term exploit is used when talking about manipulating people, whether it is with phishing or any other type of social engineering attack.

Web-based threats

There are also some attacks that use websites as the platform for the attack. These are mainly technical in nature and there is little the user can do to prevent this. The main way these attacks are prevented is by the website designer applying security to the web page, such as input validation. Cross site scripting, cross site request forgery and SQL injection are examples of web-based attacks.

These attacks will see the user being taken to another website within the session. For example, if an online marketplace suffered a cross site scripting attack, when a user clicks to go to the payment site they are taken to a different site, which resembles the genuine payment site, to enter their details, resulting in the attacker obtaining their payment card details. Unfortunately, there are a limited number of things users can do to detect they have been led to a false site, unless they are a regular visitor and know the site in great detail. The main things that can be done are checking the address of the site and also the security credentials, such as the digital certificate. These aspects are covered in Chapter 8.

Low technical threats – keyboards

There are a couple of low-level technical attacks that are both based on the keyboard you use on your home system.

Keyloggers

A keylogger is a small USB device that is plugged into the USB cable for the keyboard. The keylogger captures the first characters that are typed in a session. The number of characters that are captured varies between devices, but will be enough to capture both the username and password, although there might be some limitations if more users begin to use longer passphrases.

The attacker will need physical access to your computer to put the keylogger in place, and would also need access to the computer in the future to remove the keylogger.

Although a keylogger is a low technical threat, it still requires a degree of sophistication because the attacker has to get access to your computer. Unless the keylogger is used by someone with access to the home (such as parents monitoring children, domestic abusers monitoring their victims or home controllers who want full control of the home environment) the attacker must force or manipulate access to the computer.

It is wise to check the rear of the computer system occasionally for devices that you have not put there. This would be a good action if you feel there is a threat to you, if you have had work done in your home by an unknown person or even every couple of months for peace of mind.

Skype and type

It has been suggested that keys on keyboards create unique notes when pressed, described as 'acoustic signatures' or 'sound signatures'. Researchers have proven that these sounds could be recorded and analysed to identify keys pressed. It is very unlikely that this type of technology or attack would be used against home owners, but it cannot be ruled out.

To prevent this attack, it is advised that video-chat applications such as Skype or Facetime are not used while using the keyboard. If you were doing work or accessing a sensitive account, you could be typing a username and password, which could be recorded and analysed to reveal what was typed.

Precautions

As a home, domestic and/or personal user in the digital world there are a number of precautions you can take to protect your computer and make it harder for malware to get onto your system and damage your information:

- ✓ Use antivirus software.
- ✓ Install a host-based firewall.
- ✓ Use a spam filter.
- ✓ Use an ad-blocker.
- ✓ Set automatic regular updates.

These are technical things that can be done to protect your system but the very basic message is that the malware needs to get into your device in the first place. It is your awareness and control of this that will prevent the malware accessing your device in the first place.

What can you do?

There are plenty of things you can do to manage the risk and avoid becoming a victim. Prevent and protect are underpinned by having a security awareness mindset. The best way to achieve this is to adopt a straightforward approach: **think twice, click once!**

Prevent

The most effective way to prevent becoming a victim of cyber crime is to understand the threat and how you might be attacked.

Unfortunately, there are many ways an attacker could try to attack you online and get your information. The main thing you can do to prevent this is to apply as much security as you can. Security must make sense! If the security control is so stringent that you have to disable it to achieve routine tasks then it has no benefit. If the security control can do its job without affecting you then it has the greatest value. Also there is no single security solution: security is achieved by applying many controls, each of which adds another layer to the 'security blanket'.

For example, if your laptop was left on a coffee table while you visited the toilet, a thief might consider taking it but it is less likely they would do so if the laptop had a Kensington lock chain fitted, a screen lock visible and if the device is encrypted (as could be stated on the screen lock). While they may not get caught taking the laptop, there would be no value in a laptop with a damaged case and that requires a password to access encrypted files they can't read. The majority of thieves who would take the laptop may not have the technical knowledge or skills to overcome the password and/or encryption.

Protect

Use technical protective measures and manage your digital presence. There is no single solution to stay safe, but doing lots of small things combine into a greater security shield, awareness and posture.

Protect is in two forms, the first is by using the preventative measures as detailed above and applying a security blanket to the things you want to protect. The security blanket is a notional term which is achieved by using physical security, personal security and logical security controls.

The second measure is by knowing what information you have to protect and being very careful with that information. For example, passwords and passphrases give access to your online accounts and/or information so do not write these down, especially in plain view near the computer for example. Another example might be some pictures you want to keep private, you might store these pictures in a password protected folder (see section 5.1).

A primary aspect of protect is to regularly review your security controls and your profile security. A review every three months would be good practice.

Deter and detect

Deterrence is achieved by managing your digital presence to keep your private life private from the Internet and the world.

Detection is the recovery. There will be times when your information may have been compromised, so the detect element is to appreciate this, manage the impact and reduce how damaging this may be.

One element of detection is to know if your information may have been made available to attackers through the breach or compromise of a company. The website 'Have I been pwned?' could be used to check this. The caveat is that there may have been breaches or compromises that were not reported or even not discovered.

Have I been pwned?

www.haveibeenpwned.com is a website that searches databases of known compromised accounts from data breaches to indicate whether your email or username has been compromised in a data breach. In July 2017 the website referenced the data from 227 pwned websites, accounting for nearly four billion pwned accounts.

To find out if your email or surname has ever been pwned in a data breach, enter your name or email address in the input bar and click 'pwned?'

The results will show when the website you were registered with was breached.

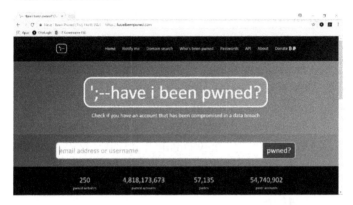

Some notable breaches in recent years have included LinkedIn, Adobe, LeapFrog, Equifax and Sony.

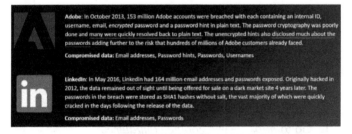

These data breaches are the sources of email addresses that are then used for other attacks. There are so many records breached now that a list of a million email addresses could be sold on the dark web for as little as $50.

If your email address or name has been pwned then in all probability it will be available to attackers, so you will probably receive phishing emails, spam and other unwanted approaches online.

What to do

If your email has been pwned, there are limited options:

1. Immediately change your password or passphrase.
2. Get a new email address, and only use the pwned email address for junk.
3. Use the pwned email address as a kind of spam filter. Do not use it for any emails that you actually want to keep.

Google Alerts

Another helpful tool is Google Alerts. This allows you to set up alerts for when new results for a topic show up on Google Search, for example your own name or the names of your children. This will not tell you when the results appear in other search engines as topic suggestions, but as Google is one of the main search engines used globally this could give you an indication.

Setting up a Google Alert is straightforward:

1. Go to *https://www.google.com/alerts.*
2. In the box at the top of the page type in the topic you want an alert about, e.g. your name.
3. Click **Show options** to set how often you receive alerts, the sources, the regions, the language, how you receive alerts and how many results you want to receive.
4. Click **Create Alert**.

You can change or delete the alerts by going to 'Show options' or selecting the alert and clicking the trashcan.

Credit Rating

There are many organisations that will enable you to check your credit rating, which is one way you can detect if you have been a victim of fraud.

Attackers are not concerned with maintaining credit rating, if they have made transactions using your credentials they will allow any agreements to expire. It is these transactions that will impact your credit rating.

When you view your credit rating you can review agreements put in place with your credentials, if you have not put these agreements in place then it's very likely this was a fraudulent agreement.

3.3 Ransomware

Petya, WannaCry and NotPetya are all strains of ransomware that had a huge, global impact on the computer systems of businesses and other organisations, including the NHS. Ransomware can also affect home users and home offices.

Ransomware is a type of malware that is delivered by social engineering. It is very different from other types of malware in terms of what it does once it is in your device or computer system. Ransomware blocks access to the information stored on the device or system, so if you have a lifetime of memories stored on your device as photographs then the ransomware could stop you viewing them, printing them or moving them to another storage device such as a USB key. The ransomware does this unless you pay a 'ransom' to the attacker, usually in an electronic currency such as bitcoin.

Many companies will tell you they have the 'solution' but these all cost money. It is possible to prevent ransomware getting in your computer in the first place, or, if it were to get into your system, to make sure only a little bit of your information is lost, all without you having to pay the 'ransom'.

The best way to make sure only the smallest amount of information is lost is to follow the backup practices that are mentioned later in this book. If ransomware were to get into your device, the easiest way to recover the system is to format the drive, reinstall the software that was initially provided with the device and reinstall your information from the backup.

Backing up weekly would be an exceptional achievement for a home user, but if you have valuable information, such as pictures of the birth of a baby, a christening or any other once-in-a-lifetime event, back up these pictures to more than one device or a memory stick, or even back them up to the Cloud.

As mentioned there is more than one way a backup can be achieved. The two primary way backups can be stored is on external hard drives or in the Cloud. There are significant differences which may influence which method is chosen.

The external hard drive is a one-off payment, is very easy to set up and the security of the information and the device is the responsibility of the owner.

The Cloud could require additional or repeat payments and there may be some additional knowledge or application required to use this method. Security of the information is entrusted in the Cloud provider.

Availability and accessibility are the main ways the Cloud is seen to be the preferred option for some. The Cloud can be accessed from any compatible device (i.e. home computer, laptop, smartphone) and can be used to backup information from any and all compatible devices, without having to connect them all to a single external hard drive. It is also possible some devices could be configured to regularly backup to the Cloud without any interaction from the user, apart from initially configuring the setting.

For some vulnerable groups, an external hard drive might be the preferred option. Some hard drives have encryption and use a PIN or password to decrypt the hard drive in order to make the information accessible. This tangible element of a hard drive is favoured for those that find the concept of the Cloud daunting or unimaginable.

By doing these things, you can recover your computer or device from a ransomware attack with no cost other than your time. Another benefit of this type of recovery is the refreshment of your computer or device: as part of the installation the computer or device will install the current updates for the operating system, Windows or iOS, as well as updates for all software and patches for hardware drivers. The computer or device will then be the best security configuration possible, before you install security tools such as antivirus, install additional software or access the Internet.

Do not worry if you are not too technical. If your computer is attacked by ransomware, you will likely have to speak to a specialist who will talk you through formatting the computer in the root configuration, which is how it needs to be rebuilt if it has been locked down by ransomware. High-street computer shops can also do this repair at a lower price than a specialist computer repairer.

It is also possible there may be a technical solution which is freely available, this will in all probability be announced on media, on social networks and also on forums. The technical solution will not be available in most cases; they are the rarity. It is advised only proven technical solutions are used, as in technical solutions that have been used by others and have been shown to work. The technical solution should only be used if you are confident you can apply it, otherwise give the device to a professional to fix.

What can you do?

- ☒ Do not pay any ransom, as there is no guarantee your information will be released or that the attackers have not left any malware on the computer or device that they could use against you in the future.
- ☑ Do backups.
- ☑ Search for and apply technical fix, if available.
- ☑ Create backups of your information
- ☑ Keep all discs and their cases (or sleeves) that came with your computer or device when you bought it as

these have the licence code for the software on or inside them so that you can reinstall in the future.

3.4 Trends

Trends are fads, actions and/or cravings that people will follow and participate in for any number of reasons, from demonstrating that the individual is 'cool' to having the opportunity to belong to a group.

Some trends have developed because digital communications such as email, mobile, etc. are more readily available, which is not necessarily a good thing. A big problem with trends is that people who are suggestible can easily be sucked into them, and when the person gets their own smartphone they have access to so many types of digital communication that it is very hard to protect them, unless they understand the possible impacts or dangers.

There are many trends that are based on inappropriate content. Most trends develop in the younger generations where there is a strong desire to 'grow up quick' or 'be an adult' before their time. The inappropriate trend generally involves some kind of sexual content or message, or a very sinister intent.

Sexting

Sexting is the sending of pictures, messages and videos with sexual content by text, computer or any other digital communication means. Sending messages that discuss or propose sexual acts is also considered sexting. There are three potentially significant issues with sexting:

1. Once a sexting message, photo or video is sent then control over the content is lost and it could end up being published. Once published it is also possible it could spread throughout the Internet.
2. What is said online, stays online. The content, be it photo, video or anything else, could haunt the person in the future.
3. In some countries, the exchange of the material may be considered child pornography or 'sextortion' and could be illegal.

The main way parents can manage this is with communication. Talk to children about the issue in such a way that they can understand that it could be dangerous for them or have an impact. Maybe use scenarios or characters to put the message in a context that children can understand. The main thing is to listen to the children's point of view and work with that as a basis. Try to get to the impact from their point of view.

Revenge porn

Revenge porn is where private explicit material is released in 'revenge'. The private explicit material might have been created when people were in a relationship that later ended; it might have been made with permission or without a person's knowledge. The basic aspect of revenge porn is that it is distributed without the consent of the person who is the subject of the material.

Revenge porn might be released because the relationship ended or in response to a comment made online or to another person.

The release of the material could be blatant, such as posting on a website or social networking site, or indirect, such as sending the material to someone who would then distribute the material.

The possible impacts on the victim can be significant, ranging from reputational impact to losing their job or even relationships.

In many countries the releasing or distributing of revenge porn is illegal.

Innocent trends

Not all trends are malicious or have bad intent. There are some trends that have become very popular. To show not everything on the Internet is bad, and also introduce these trends so that users can understand the terms I have included very quick explanations below.

These are the trends that do not have any sinister intent and allow the person following the trend to be themselves and even express themselves publicly.

Selfies

Selfies are a significant trend that has turned into common and accepted practice. A selfie can be of the person themselves or with another person. Selfies can be taken for any reason but they have become associated with social networking, being used by people to show where they are, who they are with, what they are doing, what they now look like or what they are wearing.

The selfies trend has become such an accepted social practice that there are 'selfie sticks' available for the majority of smartphones, and many smartphones now have cameras on both sides to make it simpler to take selfies.

Gifs

An animated gif is a graphic image that moves, such as a picture of a banner that waves as if the wind were ruffling it. There are gifs that are made in response to something that has happened, such as a mistake in a speech or a person crying; some gifs are popular and get circulated as a trend in their own right; and other gifs are shared by people who feel they can associate with the 'message' of the gif.

There are websites created solely for the sharing of gifs and also as gif resources; some may even charge for the gif.

Memes

A meme is an activity, catchphrase, concept or some other type of media that spreads across the Internet. The meme may be animated and could refer to anything. They can be circulated because they are humorous, convey a message or sentiment, or show a person making a mistake – basically anything could be the subject of a meme. Emojis are a type of meme that are used to communicate the way the sender is feeling, or even their opinion on something. Memes were originally sent by email, but as digital communication has developed so has the way memes are shared and what they are used for.

A meme can evolve in its design or concept, so something that originally meant one thing could be used to portray something else. The basis of a meme is that it is something 'altered by human creativity', or rather 'hijacking an original idea'.

Activities

Some trends are activities or actions, or become part of a person's character.

Cyberstalking

Cyberstalking is using the Internet or any other digital communication to 'stalk' or harass a person or group of people. Stalking can mean different things to different people: children might see stalking as following their idols or celebrities online through social media, whereas other children might consider their parents following them online as stalking.

A significant issue with cyberstalking is that it could escalate into a far more sinister activity, such as physical stalking. Victims of domestic abuse are frequently victims of cyberstalking.

Cyberstalking can be extremely invasive and upsetting for the person who is being stalked. It could be carried out by friends or family members, which could destroy those relationships, even when there was no intent to stalk the person in the first place. What is the difference between following someone's online activity and cyberstalking them?

Cyberstalking could absorb the stalker, who might then use other technology to increase their access to the victim. Possible escalations include hacking the victim's online accounts, hacking their webcam, or using 'keyloggers' to get more information (see chapter 3.2).

In many countries cyberstalking is illegal in its own right or is illegal under traditional stalking laws.

To prevent cyberstalking:

- ☑ Secure your devices by using the built-in security tools and any other such tools available. Regularly check the security of the device(s) to make sure the security is the best it can be and use security scans to make sure the device has not been breached.
- ☑ Check the physical aspects of your device to make sure nothing has been attached that shouldn't be there. Understand what software should be on the device and identify any software that shouldn't be there or that you never installed.
- ☑ Use privacy settings in your accounts to manage how much other people can see about you, your activities, your plans or your family members.
- ☑ Manage your security information to access accounts, use strong passwords or passphrases, do not use the same one repeatedly for multiple accounts, change them regularly, and don't tell anyone your passwords or passphrases.
- ☑ Regularly search your own name or your family members' names online.
- ☑ Talk to your family about your concerns. A lot of information about you could be seen through your family's, friends' or other connections' posts that you might be 'tagged' in.

Internet addiction

Internet addiction is another trend that has developed with the availability of digital devices. An Internet addict is a person who compulsively checks the Internet, whether it is social networking sites or any other media. Internet addiction is loosely described as an addiction when it interferes with everyday life, such as prioritising interacting with the Internet over normal practices in life.

Another term for Internet addiction is 'problematic Internet usage', which describes needing the Internet over normal life tasks. The comparison in everyday life is with Maslow's Hierarchy of Needs, which prioritised the human needs to function and the development of those needs as they develop in life. The contrast is that the Internet, the battery and the connectivity are all being added almost before basic life needs such as food, water and shelter. This is shown in Figure 1. Think about how many people you know that check their social media accounts before they get out of bed in the morning.

Internet addiction has been divided into four categories:

1. Information overload – too much online surfing leads to less productivity in life or at work, and impacts family relationships.
2. Cybersex addiction – too much surfing of online porn impacts real-life relationships.
3. Compulsions – spending too much time on online activities such as gambling, stocks or gaming leads to problems at work and overspending.

4. Cyber-relationship addiction – excessive use of the Internet to create relationships in contrast to time spent creating real-life relationships.

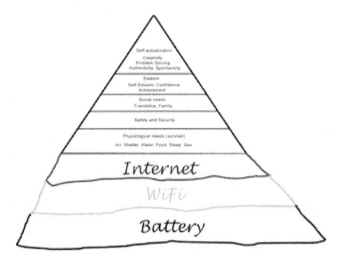

Figure 1: 21ˢᵗ Century Maslow's hierarchy of needs
(*https://twitter.com/valaafshar/status/547201974828290048*)

As with any other addiction this needs to be treated by a professional or with professional support.

3.5 Summary

What can you do, or what do you need?

There is no technological defence against social engineering. The only real defence is suspicion: be sceptical and remember that if something appears to be too good to be true then it probably is.

You are not being targeted specifically. The email is the net and some people will be victims, which is what the attacker is banking on.

As long as you avoid being an easy target, the attacker will pass over you and seek easier targets!

There are a number of habits anyone can develop that will make it harder for social engineering attacks to succeed:

- ☑ At the start of a telephone call get the caller to give you their name and number, then either call them back on a confirmed number or set a time for them to call back. Or tell the caller that it is not a convenient time and call the official number for the organisation, or the police to report your concerns.

- ☒ Do not trust caller ID because the source telephone number may be 'spoofed' – copied from a genuine number.

- ☑ If the caller professes to be from an organisation that you frequent, such as your bank, take them through a security check process, such as asking them to identify your primary branch or the name of your branch manager. Remember to ask for information that is not easily found on the Internet.

- ☑ If you live close to your bank or are due to visit there soon, state that you would prefer to provide the information in-branch. It is always possible that the attacker has discovered or been provided with information that could be used to verify identity.

- ☑ Scrutinise emails for these three things:

1. Sender's address – this should be a company or official address.
2. Spelling and grammar – a significant number of phishing attacks stem from overseas where English is not the first language.
3. Content – the email directs you to click an embedded link that will seek information, such as a bank asking you to confirm your financial information, or an online provider asking you to verify your account and access information.

☒ Do not respond to the initial approach. Open a new conversation channel (by telephone, email, personally or even by letter) to confirm the approach.

☑ Support vulnerable groups by continually reminding them of the threat and/or challenging on their behalf. Vulnerable groups might include people who have not been exposed to the dark side of human nature, such as children, or people from a former generation where trust was second nature, so avoid delivering this support in a condescending manner.

CHAPTER 4: OPERATING SYSTEM – COMPUTERS AND LAPTOPS

To protect yourself online you must understand your environment. The environment is the space in which you are operating – in this instance, the operating system.

What follows is a very brief overview of the primary operating systems used by the private user.

Many other operating systems exist, such as Java, Linux, etc., but these are primarily associated with programming, specialists and commercial environments.

The majority of the content in this book is based on Windows because it's the primary operating system in the majority of households, but the concepts, types of attacks and motivations are pretty much the same across all operating systems.

4.1 MacOS

The Macintosh is a suite of systems made by Apple with a unique operating system, macOS. The Apple Mac is a top-end device that is associated with specific tasks such as graphic design. Macs are preferred by Apple-aficionados, those who need to use them for the associated specialist applications and those who have great regard for security. The Apple Mac was traditionally regarded as an infallible platform because few viruses targeted it, mainly because there were a lot less users as the computers tend to be very expensive, compared to other computers. The Mac now appears to be popular enough to draw the virus-writers' attention. It is being reported more frequently now that vulnerabilities do exist and exploits have been discovered.

Setting the privacy and security on a Macintosh device is the main way to manage the information that your computer shares about you.

The following five images show how to configure the security settings on a Mac for the most effective level of security.

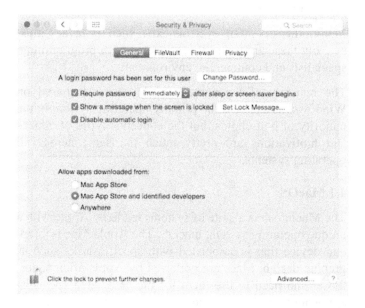

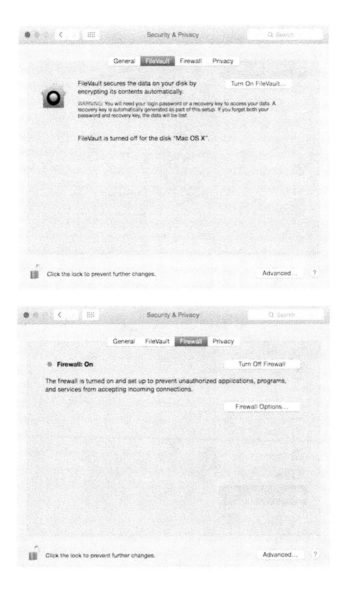

Security resources for macOS

Devices running macOS are not immune to viruses and attacks, but there is far less malware in circulation than there is for Windows. There are some specialist security applications that can be used to protect your Mac, but before you consider installing any of them, make sure you do the basics:

☑ Allow automatic updates.
☑ Turn the firewall on.
☑ Encrypt your data.

Antivirus

Some antivirus apps are listed below, with the free ones first.

Avast!

Free Mac security – *www.avast.com*.

Malwarebytes

Malwarebytes Anti-Malware for Mac is free – *www.malwarebytes.com*.

There is another resource called Malwarebytes 3, which is a multi-layer solution that must be paid for.

Sophos

Sophos Home: free protection for home computers – *www.sophos.com*.

There are a number of mostly free applications for home security, but one or two require a subscription or a purchase.

Avira

Free antivirus software for Mac – *www.avira.com*.

The aforementioned antivirus sites have numerous security resources for Macs. The two types of security tools that should be used are web security and a VPN.

4.2 Windows

Microsoft Windows is undoubtedly the most widely used operating system in the private, commercial and public sectors. Microsoft Windows is the firm favourite in the commercial sector and public sector as it can be used for enterprises, from organisations operating in close-knit environments such as offices, to those operating globally with offices worldwide. It is the preferred operating system in the private sector because it is affordable and for most it is the easier system to use. It is used in schools as the preferred teaching platform as it is the operating system used in most offices.

It is for these reasons, Windows being the enterprise office system and the most widely used home operating system, that it is the favoured target for attackers!

The first way your system can be protected is by using the latest version of Windows. At the time of writing, the current Microsoft operating system is Windows 10. Out-of-date operating systems and software no longer get updates from the manufacturer to protect against current threats and so they are vulnerable to malware.

Security resources for Windows

There are so many security resources available on the Internet that it is hard to know which are right for you, which work together and which are easy to use. Many companies offer free versions of their security tools, with extra functions at a cost, which is usually a licence that has to be renewed annually.

By paying for a security tool or suite you could have a single solution that can manage a number of security aspects, but it is possible to achieve the same level of security by using multiple free resources. These free resources then need to be managed individually and coordinated.

Most of the free resources are designed for network administrators and managers, but some can be useful for home users.

When searching for 'free windows security tools' one of the first results may be 'The Windows Club' (*www.thewindowsclub.com*). The Windows Club is an unofficial forum which is a good reference, but the actual software should only be downloaded from official Microsoft websites, go to *www.support.microsoft.com.*

Three free security tools for home users are listed below.

Windows Defender Offline

This is a malware identification tool that dives deep into the root of the operating system and removes malware that the majority of security tools would not be able to identify. When the tool identifies any malware it creates an alert to inform you and lets you decide whether to delete or quarantine the malware.

Windows Defender Offline is a good tool as it inspects the root of your system before the system even uses it.

This tool is also equipped with Microsoft Active Protection Service (MAPS), which informs Microsoft if it encounters any malware, enabling Microsoft to develop a fix that is then released for other Windows users in an update.

Microsoft Safety Scanner

Microsoft Safety Scanner is an on-demand scanner, which means you must instruct it to scan your system. The tool will ask what type of scan you want to launch: quick scan, full scan or customised scan. The customised scan will only scan the specific files or types of files you direct. The best option is the full scan because it inspects the whole system, although it is the slowest and longest type.

This is not a free resource in the truest sense: the tool is free for the first ten days but then a licence is required that must be paid for.

Malicious Software Removal Tool

This is another scanner from Microsoft that removes specific prevalent malware. This tool will work on Windows operating systems from Vista onwards.

Full information on all these tools is available from each individual download page.

FileHippo – the free downloads site

Many free security resources for Windows are available at *www.filehippo.com*. There are ratings and reviews for each application and a number of different categories, each with a number of applications available for download by home users. Table 1 lists the ten most relevant resources in four key categories. The best practice would be to use FileHippo as a reference site, only downloading tools from the manufacturers' websites, i.e. only download Avira antivirus software from *www.avira.com*.

Table 1: FileHippo resources

Security	Anti-malware	System tuning	File transfer
Comodo Internet Security	Avast! Free Antivirus	3DMark Vantage	FileZilla
SunBelt Personal Firewall	Avira Free Antivirus	Autoruns	FlashGet
SyGate Personal Firewall	CWShredder	CCleaner	GMailDrive
ZoneAlarm Free Firewall	GridinSoft Anti-malware	Defraggler	Internet Download Manager
360 Total Security Essential	HiJackThis	Process Explorer	TeraCopy
Abelssoft Anti Logger	Rootkit Revealer	Sandra Lite	4shared Desktop

Security	Anti-malware	System tuning	File transfer
Advanced Password Manager	SpyBot Search and Destroy	Speccy	Binfer
Anvi Folder Locker Free	Spyware Blaster	3DMark 11	Connect2
Ashampoo Privacy Protector	Windows Defender	3DMark Windows Basic Edition	Copy Handler
AxCrypt	360 Total Security Free Antivirus	3DMark03	Core FTP LE

Table 2: Other groups on FileHippo and the top tools in each group by relevance

Networking	Photo/image	File sharing	Compression
Hamachi	FastStone	eMule	Recuva
RealVNC	Image Viewer	FrostWire	SyncBack
TeamViewer	Paint.Net	uTorrent	WinZip
360	ACDSee	Vuze	7-Data Card
TurboVPN	Adobe	Ares	Recovery
Acrylic Wifi	Creative	Galaxy	7-zip
Home	Cloud	Bearshare	Abelssoft
Advanced IP	Adobe	Bearshare	Backup
scanner	Creative	Life	Abelssoft
Aircrack-ng	Cloud	BitComet	Undeleter
Android-x86	Photography	BitTorrent	Acronis True
Angry IP	Ant Renamer	BitTorrent	Image 2017
scanner	AVS Image	Sync	Android data
AnyDesk	Converter		Recovery Pro

Networking	Photo/image	File sharing	Compression
	AVS Photo Editor Axialis IconWorkshop Blender		Any Data Recovery Pro

CHAPTER 5: HOME OFFICE

The term 'home office' describes three concepts:

1. Every business or home enterprise must start somewhere, usually with a home office.
2. Many households might manage their home through a single room, which by default becomes the home office.
3. When people work remotely they tend to work in their home office.

A home office is usually regarded as the highest priority for the household's Internet access, so the router would be located there as well as the printer, the desktop and any other network aspects.

Where the home office is used as the foundation for a home enterprise or small business, it is even more critical, but it is also the likely target for attackers who know that users and small businesses tend not to commit large budgets to information or cyber security. As well as the expense, there is the time commitment required to develop a robust security posture.

As a rule, the majority of free resources are available to home users but there tends to be a restriction if it is for commercial use. Where it is legal to do so, the majority of resources in this book can be applied to home office and home network use, especially as the majority of home office networks and home networks will generally be built using Windows.

There is no minimum or maximum set for how much security is secure. The best approach would be to apply as much of the security guidance in this book as possible. If there are any conflicts or difficulties in the system that stop you working, only reduce the security aspects as little as you possibly can to allow you to work.

The five basic requirements for the home office are:

1. Remove unnecessary applications and services from the device, including the webcam, microphone, etc. where they aren't explicitly needed
2. Set up automatic updates and patches.
3. Install anti-malware and antivirus software, set up a firewall, etc.
4. Change any default passwords and only give users on the system permission to do what they need to do. Not everyone needs to be an administrator.
5. Install web security tools and use trusted online services such as email.

5.1 Home office and home networks

The home network can connect all the devices in the home, be they personal computing devices, smartphones, printers, a fridge, lightbulbs or even a hairbrush. The home network is an invaluable resource in the modern home, connecting the home to the residents whether they are in the house or away. The home network is the hub that consolidates all the resources, but if its security is not managed then it can also be the single point of failure for those resources.

Network encryption

A significant aspect of the security is the network encryption. At the very least, Advanced Encryption Standard (AES) should be used; better would be Wi-fi Protected Access 2 (WPA2). These can be configured when setting up the network router.

Network SSID

The network SSID is the name of the network that is displayed by the router. It is the name that is displayed when you search wireless networks in range. A very basic security measure you can do for network security is to give the network an SSID that does not identify it as your network, such as HomeNetworkOne, instead of giving the network a name associated with you, such as Joe'sHome.

Network password/passphrase

The network password is the key to the home network. The network password should be very robust and regularly changed. Best practice would be to use a passphrase that is easily remembered. Guidance on passwords and passphrases is included later in this section.

Network firewall

Most routers have a robust firewall built in and additional features include network address translation, which is another way to mask the devices in your home network. Other free home network firewalls include ZoneAlarm (*www.zonealarm.com*) and Comodo (*www.personalfirewall.comodo.com*). Another option is OpenDNS (*www.opendns.com*), which is not a firewall per se but modifies your router settings so that it connects through OpenDNS servers. By connecting in this way, OpenDNS protects all connected devices in your home network.

Network security suite

A significant extension to the home network security is the Sophos Home security suite, which provides "Free business-grade security for your home Macs and PCs". It is available from *www.home.sophos.com*.

Another option is Sophos UTM Home Edition (UTM is unified threat management). This is a significant commitment to security as it requires a computer dedicated to the application, which will become a fully functional security appliance. The application is available from *www.sophos.com*.

Vulnerability assessment

A vulnerability assessment is a very effective tool for home networks. It scans the network based on the IP address and identifies any known vulnerabilities. One potential issue with commercial vulnerability assessments is that they are more oriented to compliance and commercial environments than to home networks.

A number of companies offer free vulnerability assessments that indicate the status of the home network. Best practice would be to launch a vulnerability assessment monthly and use the resulting report to remediate any identified vulnerabilities.

Network attached storage – personal Cloud

Network attached storage is generally referred to as a 'personal Cloud'. The Cloud is a network of computers that can be accessed over the Internet. Information in the Cloud is not literally held in the atmosphere like a white fluffy cloud; rather, it is held on a physical computer located somewhere in the world.

A personal Cloud is an extension of the home system, basically being additional storage for the home network that can be accessed through the Internet. The security of the service is defined by the administrator of the home system.

Windows Defender

Windows Defender is malware protection that was built into Windows 8. The software helps identify and remove viruses, spyware and other malicious software. Windows Defender has a default configuration that is the Microsoft common settings. Windows Defender should be the basic security measure for any home device, but it should be configured to meet the user's specific needs.

Firewall – info only

A firewall is a device that can be applied to a computer to restrict the traffic gaining access to it from the Internet. Most people have heard of firewalls as this term is bounded about in the media extensively. Firewalls are found in commercial networks more so than home networks.

Firewalls can be difficult to configure and generally require a repetitive payment. Some providers allow the firewall to be downloaded for free, but then require a fee to be paid to maintain it.

By using an effective Antivirus and other tools mentioned in this book, a comparable level of security would be achieved to that of a network using firewalls.

Antivirus

Antivirus software is essential for all users. There are four things that must be considered when deciding on antivirus software:

1. How regularly the application is updated.
2. How easy the application is to use.
3. What management tools are available when detections are made.
4. How the application engages with the system.

The free Avira and AVG antivirus software are regularly updated, have easy user interfaces, and allow you to quarantine or remove any potential virus that is detected.

Norton antivirus lost favour with professionals as it engaged with the system registry and made changes that could make it more difficult to install alternative antivirus software in the future.

There are many free antivirus applications for home users, some of which are listed at *www.filehippo.com*. You could also search 'free home antivirus' and most search engines will return a number of results, each of which would likely be significantly better than having no antivirus.

Many providers are developing their free resources into security suites that combine a number of features. These suites put the antivirus at the core, with functions such as ad blocker, spam filter and Internet security added as necessary.

Passwords

Passwords are generally the primary means of authenticating a user seeking to access a protected or secure site or application. As the understanding of password frailty develops more users are acknowledging complexity requirements and making passwords more secure by applying some basic rules:

- Password length should be, at the very least, between six and eight characters.
- Passwords should contain a mixture of letters, numbers and special characters. Special characters are the characters accessed by using the shift key with the number keys, i.e. !"£$%^&*().
- Passwords should have upper and lower case letters.
- Different passwords should be used to access different sites. This way, if the password for one site is compromised, access to accounts you might have on other sites will not be affected.
- Passwords for different sites should not follow the same sequence and be easy to guess, e.g. if your password for Facebook is 'TimpwfFB', don't then use 'TimpwfSC' for Snapchat.

- Passwords should not be made up of personal information that people could easily guess, such as names and dates of birth.

A good process for generating unique passwords is to associate the password with the site and use alternative characters to represent letters; for example:

This is the password for my Barclays current account

may be read as

This !s the pass word 4 my Barclays current account

which would be entered on the keyboard as *T!tpw4mBca*

It is possible to replace letters you might use in a password with alternative characters. You are not restricted to one character for each letter, as shown in Table 3.

Table 3: Alternative characters

A	Aa@	G	Gg	M	Mm	S	Ss5	Y	Yy
B	Bb6	H	Hh	N	Nn	T	Tt	Z	Zz
C	Cc	I	Ii1!	O	Oo0	U	Uu		
D	Dd	J	Jj	P	Pp	V	Vv		
E	Ee3€	K	Kk	Q	Qq	W	Ww		
F	Ff	L	Ll	R	Rr	X	Xx		

Most commonly used passwords

Every year, there are surveys that reveal the most common passwords, and every year the cyber security community groans because the same passwords appear again and again, despite efforts to get people to use stronger passwords. The following passwords are recovered from the millions of passwords that are compromised each year and made public. Table 4 lists the top 20 most commonly used passwords for 2014, 2015 and 2016.

Table 4: Top 20 commonly used passwords

	2014	2015	2016
1	123456	123456	123456
2	password	password	123456789
3	12345	12345678	qwerty
4	12345678	qwerty	12345678
5	qwerty	12345	111111
6	123456789	123456789	1234567890
7	1234	football	1234567
8	baseball	1234	password
9	dragon	1234567	123123
10	football	baseball	987654321
11	1234567	welcome	qwertyuiop
12	monkey	1234567890	mynoob
13	letmein	abc123	123321
14	abc123	111111	666666
15	111111	1qaz2wsx	18atcskd2w

	2014	2015	2016
16	mustang	dragon	7777777
17	access	master	1q2w3e4r
18	shadow	monkey	654321
19	master	letmein	555555
20	michael	login	3rjs1la7qe

There are trends with these passwords that have made them easy for attackers to breach. The requirement for separate passwords for different accounts has led to users repeating passwords across different accounts, which again makes it easy for attackers. These reasons have made using passphrases current best practice.

Passphrases

A passphrase is a group of words combined to create a longer password. The passphrase should ideally have at least 14 characters. Passphrases are harder to breach than passwords because they have so many more characters, and including special characters can make it even harder to breach them. Special characters are detailed in Passwords.

As with passwords, the same passphrase should not be used for multiple accounts. Using a password wallet would make it easier to manage multiple passphrases, or associate the passphrase with the account but avoid using a repeated sequence to keep it difficult to breach.

Don't use similar strands of passphrases for different sites, e.g. if your passphrase for Facebook is 'iusefacebooktochattofriends', don't use 'iusetwittertotweettomyfriends' for Twitter.

Password strength

Many companies provide a way to show you how strong your password is. One good site is *www.howsecureismypassword.net*, as it also shows how much better a passphrase may be than a password.

For example, the site suggests it would take a computer eight months to crack the password 'LadyGodiva'. If a couple of characters in the same password were replaced with special characters to read 'LadyG0d!va', it would take the computer six years to crack.

The passphrase 'LadyGodivarodeahorse' would take a computer 17 quadrillion years to crack – 17,000,000,000,000,000,000 years.

Password wallet

A password wallet is an application that stores all of a person's passwords securely. The two main things to remember with a password wallet is to have a very secure unique password or passphrase to access the wallet, and keep a secure record of the password or passphrase, such as in the home safe, or in a hidden file on a computer, or even written down masked in a sentence that only you would recognise.

Password sheet

A low-level alternative to a password wallet is an encrypted password sheet. In a household with two adult members the option remains to provide mutual support and security using a password sheet, which of course is built on a foundation of mutual trust as potentially each person has access to the other's sites and accounts.

The password sheet can be generated as a Word document. The document is a straightforward table with three or four columns: site, username, password and comment. The 'comment' column can be used to record the date the password was changed or any other pertinent information.

Mutual security is achieved by recording the passwords for adult A on the sheet of Adult B and vice-versa. It is improbable that both adults will forget the passwords for their password sheets at the same time.

For guidance on how to encrypt a Word document go to Help in the application. When applying a password to a document make sure it is required to both read and modify.

Multi-factor authentication

Multi-factor authentication is an option that is available with many accounts. Wherever possible you should use it. If an account has this option, it would be in the security settings of the account.

Multi-factor authentication is when you use something you have to verify your identity when accessing an online account. For example, when using an online marketplace such as Amazon your bank might require you to verify your transaction. You have used your credentials to access the online marketplace - before the transaction is approved the bank might send a text message to your mobile phone, which verifies it is you making the transaction.

This is multi-factor as the security credentials to access the online marketplace is one factor, *something you know*, and the text message to your smartphone, *something you have*, is the second factor.

There is another authentication factor that is used, on iPhones for example, which is your fingerprint, *something you are*.

Screen lock

The screen lock is a way to prevent access to the information on the computer if you have to move away from the device for any period of time. The screen lock is explained in 'Mobile security' (section 6.1).

Webcams

A potential vulnerability has been identified in webcams, which can allow attackers to access and control them. Once an attacker has access to the webcam they could potentially get access throughout the system, as well as gain extra information that could be used in a social engineering attack.

✓ Disable or disconnect the webcam.
✓ Cover the webcam lens with tape.

Another risk with webcams is ambient activity or ambient noise, which basically means background activity or noise. Anything that happens within view of the webcam when it is on is transmitted, as well as anything that is said. When using webcams be conscious of this risk, maybe go into a private area or an area where there will be fewer people or background noise.

Parental settings

Parental settings are another way to manage Internet access from the home computer or other devices. Parental settings are explored later in the 'Parental security' section.

Parental settings are available to protect people who might need help and guidance to stay protected or safe on the Internet. They can also be used to protect members of other vulnerable groups, but they might need to be explained differently or even put in place when the person's account is initially built.

Family account

Another way to manage how the family uses the home computer is by building a family account on Microsoft. A family account is marketed as 'One place to manage your account'. You can manage the security and privacy of the device and users with a single family account, as well as many other tasks, such as viewing browsing history and reviewing purchase history. To set up a family account go to account.microsoft.com/family.

Administrator account

The administrator account is the prime target for all attackers as it allows unrestricted access throughout the system. There are some basic actions that can protect the administrator account.

By default, the first account built on a system is the administrator account, so do not name it 'admin' or 'administrator', name it something different that would not make it obvious to an attacker. If the admin or administrator accounts do exist, remove the administrator privileges and move these to an account that is not named anything relating to the administrator role. That way, if an attacker does get into the network they might attack the wrong account.

The administrator account should only be used for administrator tasks; it should not be used for routine tasks as mistakes could happen. If a mistake is made in a normal account it could affect only one user, if it is made in the administrator account it could affect all users of the computer.

The passphrase of the admin account should be very strong as it protects the admin rights of the computer. It will be the main target for the attacker, so should have a password or passphrase that is very difficult to break.

Updates

Updates are issued by manufacturers and providers of software, hardware and firmware. Updates are often used to resolve potential vulnerabilities that have been identified.

It is possible that updates may cause a conflict within the system, either between software applications or in the configuration of the system. Best practice would be to ensure that a backup of the system is created before updates are applied.

To manage this process, do the following:

1. Set a backup of the whole system to be created at 2:00 am every Wednesday.

2. Set the backup to be created at a location other than the system that is being backed up.
3. Set updates to be downloaded and applied at 4:00 am every Wednesday.

Should the updates subsequently cause an issue, it will be possible to restore the backup and restore the system to the configuration before the updates were applied.

If an update does cause an issue, you will need to manage the actual installation of the update, potentially delaying it until a fix is available. It is possible to discover any issues with updates or when fixes are available by using the appropriate terms in a search engine.

One thing Windows operating systems up to Windows 7 allowed you to do was define a restore point before any configuration or operating system changes were made. You can use a restore point to return the device or operating system to a 'good' configuration before an update was applied that conflicted with the configuration.

If Restore is not available, then the system will allow you to Reset. This allows you to manage the files that are available on the system and re-installs Windows. By using Reset you could remove the file that caused a conflict, which ultimately caused the system to freeze.

These 'tools' are found through the Control Panel.

Patches

Patches are for hardware as updates are for software: they are the manufacturer's duty of care to continually review the effectiveness of the configuration and security of their devices to protect users – and to protect the manufacturer's reputation.

Firmware

Firmware is the software built directly into the physical hardware rather than as part of or within the operating system. Because firmware isn't meant to change, these patches are generally only issued for especially important security updates.

Removable media

Removable media is any media that can be used to transfer information from one device to another, such as USB keys, CDs, tapes, etc. Here are a few basic things to remember:

- ✓ Do not use any removable media that you find on the floor or lying around.
- ✓ Format any removable media before you use it (see section 6.6).
- ✓ Fully encrypt any removable device where possible.

If an attacker cannot get physical access to the information on the removable media, it cannot be exploited.

There is a free application to encrypt USB storage devices available from *www.filehippo.com*.

Another option is to use a USB device that has a PIN that must be entered to unlock the data on the device. One such device is available from *www.myistorage.co.uk*. An example of the device can be seen in the following image.

5.2 Computer disposal

When you are looking to replace your computer or just selling it on, you need to make sure it is only the computer you are passing on, not your personal information as well. If you are selling the computer, you want the system to be in a working condition so you can get the best deal. The easiest way to do this is to format the computer by reinstalling the operating system. Another way is to take the computer to a computer technician who could format the device using DOS.

If you are destroying the device, the best thing to do is open the computer, remove the hard drive and destroy this with a hammer. This makes sure that there is very little chance any information on the hard drive could be recovered and used against you. To make absolutely sure, format the computer first, which will take time but will make sure no information can be recovered.

If the computer stops working and you are not able to format the drive, the best thing to do is destroy the hard drive with a hammer. The shell of the computer should then be taken to a recycling depot where the parts will be disposed of according to the law.

CHAPTER 6: MOBILE SECURITY

When you are mobile you are at your weakest as you are operating in insecure environments. At home you know you have security on your device and your network; when you are mobile you rely on the security put in place by the Internet access provider, which is usually a lower priority than availability.

Mobile devices need to be manageable because they need to be mobile, which also means they are easier to snatch from a laptop bag or from a table in a coffee shop.

6.1 Laptop

The security of laptops is primarily achieved by how the device is configured and the software that is installed. This is covered in the 'Operating system – computers and laptops' section.

Laptops need extra security because they are designed to be portable, so the main requirements are to prevent them being stolen, to protect the information on the device if it is stolen, and to protect the information while it is mobile.

Devices such as Kensington locks are very useful to prevent laptops being stolen. Encryption and backup are essential to protect your information if your device is stolen. A VPN is also essential to secure your information when you connect to Wi-Fi outside your home or regular network.

Kensington lock

The main threat to the domestic user is laptop theft. Thieves are not after the data on the laptop but the laptop itself because they can resell it. Each laptop has a Kensington port, which is a rectangular hole in the body of the laptop into which a Kensington lock can be fitted. Thieves will be less likely to steal a laptop if they can get no money for it because it is damaged, which breaking the Kensington lock will do. The Kensington lock is circled in the image below.

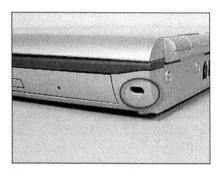

The Kensington lock will not stop the laptop being stolen, but it will break the body of the laptop and significantly reduce the value of the stolen device, to the extent the thief may see the device as valueless and not worth the potential risk or effort.

Kensington locks are available in two versions: with a key or with a combination lock.

A keyed Kensington lock fitted to secure a device:

A combination Kensington lock:

You can also use a Kensington lock to secure the laptop if you leave it in a car. Preferably put the device out of sight in the boot or use the Kensington lock to secure the device to the seat frames.

Screen filter

A basic security measure that can be applied to your laptop is a screen filter. The screen filter sits on your laptop screen and prevents someone from seeing what is displayed on the screen unless they are sat directly in front of the device as shown in the image below.

The laptop screen filter prevents a threat called 'shoulder-surfing', which is where somebody stands behind you and reads what is displayed on the screen. Screen filters are very easy to fit: they usually just sit in the screen recess on laptops with plastic guides to hold them in place.

Screen filters make the screen appear black to anyone other than the person sat directly in front of the screen.

3M is the primary manufacturer of screen filters which can be bought through Amazon or other vendors. Search 'privacy filter' and find the correct size for your device.

Screen lock

If a Windows device is not touched for any period of time, the best practice is to have a screen lock in place. The screen lock is managed through the Control Panel, under the Personalisation options.

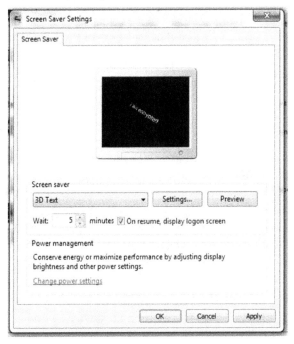

The screen saver stops access if you are away from the device, and can include a message.

The screen lock is managed through the screen saver. The screen saver can be text or a picture, and can include a message that will deter potential thieves. The text in the image above reads 'I am encrypted', which tells an attacker three things:

1. You understand security and are committed to protecting yourself and your information.
2. You have applied encryption to protect the information on the device.
3. The attacker will not have access to the information if they take the laptop.

Used in combination with a Kensington lock, the screen saver presents a number of challenges to a thief.

When configuring the screen saver, tick 'On resume display logon screen', which means the device's passphrase is required to unlock the screen. Set the time in 'Wait' by using the arrows to select the minutes – this defines the length of time the device remains unlocked and the information accessible without it being touched. The ideal period of time is three minutes. There are a number of reasons three minutes can be regarded as the ideal setting;

1. By the time an attacker got access to your laptop, three minutes would not leave much time to view or copy your information.
2. If you moved away from the device a good amount of the three minutes would have expired before the device was out of your view.
3. Three minutes would allow you enough time to do a quick task away from the device and return before the screen locked, i.e. get something from your bag, put the kettle on, etc.
4. It is unlikely most users would remember to change this setting before travelling so three

minutes would be an acceptable time setting for this circumstance as well.

You can also lock the screen if you are moving away from the device for a few minutes: press Ctrl-Alt-Delete at the same time to lock the screen and require the passphrase to open the device again. You can also hold the Windows key and 'l' to lock the screen.

6.2 Public Wi-Fi

Do not use insecure wireless Internet access because attackers may be able to intercept any information you send through the connection. Never use an insecure connection to send or access valuable information, such as financial or personal information.

If public Wi-Fi is the only option available, make sure you use a VPN.

Do not assume the Wi-Fi is secure in your hotel room or other temporary accommodation. The only indication a Wi-Fi network has any security is when a network key is required, which is a password to access the network.

Whether or not you have to use a password to access the network, best practice is to use a VPN.

The VPN gives you some security even if the network security level is weak. It is possible to check the level of security that has been applied to the network, but best practice is still to open all browsers with a VPN in place.

If you need to open a browser to access sensitive information when you are away from home, always use a VPN for the connection.

6.3 VPN

Using a VPN provides greater security when connecting to the Internet because it launches an encrypted link between the source and the destination computer. This ensures there is a secure link between your system and the destination system.

The VPN also generates an IP address that means the user's true IP address is not revealed, further reducing the possibility of being attacked.

A number of free VPN solutions can be found through FileHippo.

Once you have installed the VPN make sure you understand how to turn it on and what you need to see to show you are connecting through a VPN. Alternatively, depending on which browser and VPN solution you use, configure the browser so that it only opens in a VPN.

VPNs should be used when connecting to public networks and also when using mobile networks, whenever possible.

Mobile networks are the networks you connect to when you are 'roaming', either in your home country or overseas.

6.4 Public computers

Internet cafés are readily available in every city. Caution must be exercised when using the systems in Internet cafés as these systems are susceptible to attack by such devices as keyboard loggers or other low-tech attacks. The main thing you can do is avoid using internet cafes or any other public systems to access sensitive sites, such as your online banking.

As Internet cafés are open to the public there would be no difficulty in someone fitting and subsequently removing a keyboard logger. The attacker only has to keep reviewing the information captured by the keyboard logger until they capture the access credentials for a financial site, or your security credentials to access your online profile, or even your card details where you might have made a purchase.

6.5 USB devices

Depending on where you are travelling, new USB storage devices could have malware installed that would transfer to your device when the USB is inserted, even when they are in the manufacturer's packaging. This risk may not exist in every country you travel in, but best practice is to get in the habit of checking USB devices before you use them.

When you buy a USB storage device install a means to encrypt the key and protect the information if the key is lost or stolen. Some USB storage devices come with embedded encryption, saving you this effort.

Only buy encrypted USB keys from trusted reputable providers, such as Western Digital or Seagate.

Ensure the firmware on the device is backed up before formatting the device or that any necessary firmware is readily available from a trusted source, preferably the manufacturer's website.

I recommend formatting every USB device before it is used for the first time:

In 'Computer', left-click the device to select, right-click the device and select 'Format'.

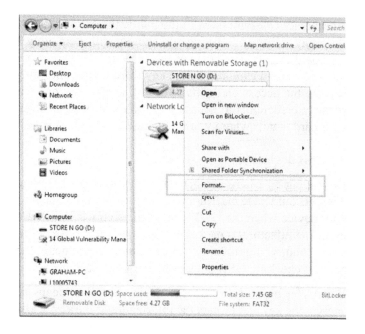

The format control panel will appear with two options:

- Quick format – erases the registry of the device, which is the index showing the location of all information on the device. Deleting this index means the information cannot be found.
- Full format – erases all data on the device.

Once the device is formatted install an encryption application for the USB storage device. There are applications for doing this at *www.filehippo.com*.

6.6 International travel

The basics of mobile security are the same wherever you are, but there may be additional advice or considerations if you are going to specific countries.

Travelling in the EU is fairly straightforward as the majority of countries are aligned with EU legislation. Other countries in the world may have different requirements, e.g. some countries restrict encryption devices being brought in.

For the most up-to-date information, check your government's travel advice for the country you are travelling to.

In Ireland, this advice is given by the Department of Foreign Affairs and Trade at *www.dfa.ie/travel/travel-advice*.

In the UK, this advice is given by the Foreign and Commonwealth Office at *www.gov.uk/foreign-travel-advice*.

EU roaming charges

Roaming charges were abolished across the EU from June 2017. This means if you have a contract with an EU mobile provider that includes data, you can use your allowance anywhere within the EU without incurring roaming charges.

From a security perspective this is very good news as you can now use your mobile data allowance to connect to the Internet through your smartphone hotspot instead of using insecure public Wi-Fi networks.

Encrypted devices

Some countries have restrictions on bringing in encrypted devices and information.

In these countries, border control staff could demand the password for the device and take the device away for a period of time. Remember that it can take as little as two minutes to copy the entire contents of a device.

There are things that can be done to reduce the amount of information that is taken or viewed if you are challenged in this way, or if you have to open the device or even give the device and the password or passphrase to border control staff.

Laptops

Have as little information on the device as possible. Consider carrying important information on a USB device that you carry separately.

If you have a personal Cloud/network attached storage device, use this to store important information and launch a VPN to access it. If you have an iCloud account, use this to access important information.

Another option is to send yourself the information in an email that you can access but is not stored on your device.

Mobile phones

If you have an older smartphone, take this with you to access the Internet over Wi-Fi, but make sure you will not need to access sensitive sites such as e-commerce, e-banking, etc.

Don't take your new smartphone with you!

As with the laptops advice, use iCloud, or send yourself the information in an email that you can access through your account.

Posture

Be comfortable, be clever!

There is no shame in wearing gloves when it is cold, no matter how hardy you are. Wearing gloves means you do not have to keep your hands in your pockets when you are walking, which not only improves your posture but also shows you are not restricted if you need to respond to an attacker. Every little action you do to deter a potential attacker can work together to make them think twice about attacking you.

6.7 Summary

There are some basic security measures you can put in place to prevent your device being stolen. If it is stolen, these measures will prevent your information from being compromised.

- ☒ Do not leave the device unattended and unsecured.
- ☒ Do not travel with your backup device and primary device together in the same bag.
- ☒ Do not use locally bought USB devices.
- ☒ Do not use USB ports to charge devices – use a travel plug and appropriate cables.
- ☒ Do not log onto public Wi-Fi networks unless you have a VPN in place.
- ☑ Do use a Kensington lock.
- ☑ Do use a screen filter.
- ☑ Do make sure your device is encrypted.
- ☑ Do install a VPN.
- ☑ Do make sure your device has a robust passphrase.
- ☑ Do have an encrypted USB to back up information or for transferring information.

☑ Do carry the power cable, travel plug and cables for charging smartphones.

☑ Use your email or a secure Cloud to store important information if you need to access it.

CHAPTER 7: SMARTPHONES AND TABLETS

Remember that a smartphone is not just a phone but a very portable computer system, as are iPads, tablets, smartwatches and any other personal smart devices. They should be managed as computers, applying the computer security described in this book.

There are two main operating systems for smartphones and tablets: iOS is the operating system for Apple iPhones and tablets, and Android is the operating system for most other smartphones and tablets. Each type of operating system has a number of configuration options to set the privacy and security for the device.

These privacy and security options can be supported by specialist software that provide extra security. This software is available from the vendor's website, from the Apple App Store or from the Google Play Store.

7.1 Apple

The iPhone is regarded as the leading smartphone. Apple has developed a niche in the smartphone arena with newly released iPhones selling out the minute they hit the shelves.

The impressive security functions of iPhones tend to be overlooked or not fully understood by users.

There are many things that can be done on an iPhone and in the applications to manage your privacy and security. The menu and options on the iPad are generally the same as those on the iPhone, so this guidance supports both devices.

Location services

Location services enables apps and websites to access data that they can use to determine your location. The services can be turned off altogether, or permitted on an app-by-app basis. Certain applications depend on location services for their functionality, so turning on or off the setting by application is best practice, rather than turning it on for all applications.

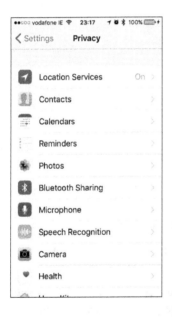

From the same menu you can choose whether to share iPhone analytics with Apple, which help its developers improve future products. The analytics will contain location information and other data so best practice is to **not** share any analytics information by turning these **off**.

Searching the web

You can change the default search engine to another search engine, and you can also turn off Safari Suggestions if you don't want the information to be sent to Apple.

Further down the page are options to control the information that Safari collects as you browse. You can turn on 'Do not track requests', but this is not guaranteed as it is down to the individual websites. You can also limit the storage of cookies on your device. Using both of these options will limit the amount of information that websites collect about you but they might affect some sites.

Selecting 'Allow from Current Website Only' will allow individual sites to work but will stop outside websites monitoring your activities.

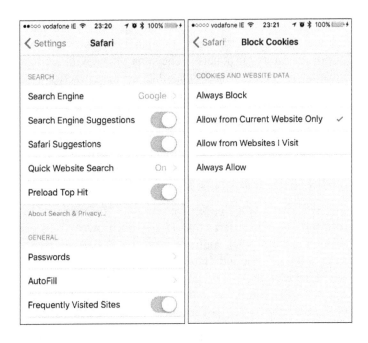

The 'Clear History and Website Data' option should be used, as this deletes all cookies and browsing information saved on your device.

Another menu in Safari's settings is 'AutoFill'. Make sure the majority of these settings are turned off otherwise the information could be saved on your device, which would make it vulnerable if your device was ever breached.

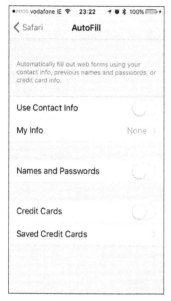

From the 'Settings' menu select 'Touch ID & Passcode'. Setting a touch ID and passcode will provide some security for your device if you lose it or someone else gets access to it. Turn on 'Auto-lock' in the 'General' menu so that the iPhone locks itself after a short period of not being used.

The more apps you install, the greater the chance that your information is not controlled, so it's best to limit the apps you have installed to those you really need, and to ensure they're kept up to date.

Apple Password hack

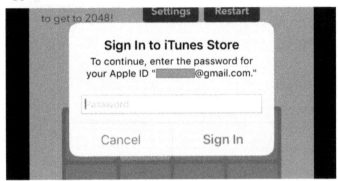

There is a recent attack that is unique to ios devices, particularly iPhones. The attack aims to get you to enter your Apple password. The attack occurs by displaying the Password required dialogue box, as seen below.

The only way to determine if this is an attack or a genuine request from the device is to press the 'Home' button. If it is an attack the dialogue box will disappear, if it is a genuine requirement then only entering the password or using 'Cancel' will close the dialogue box.

7.2 Android

The majority of smartphones run on the Android operating system, but the built-in security functions on Android devices are not as robust as those on iPhones.

Location permissions

You can turn location permissions on or off for individual apps. Go to the 'Settings' app, tap 'Apps', tap the gear icon and tap 'Location permissions'.

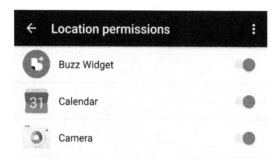

Google settings

Google is embedded in the Android operating system. There are some controls you can apply in the 'Google Now' app in the app drawer. Tap 'Menu' and then 'Settings'. From here you can manage the data Google collects about you and how you use your smartphone, ranging from location to search history.

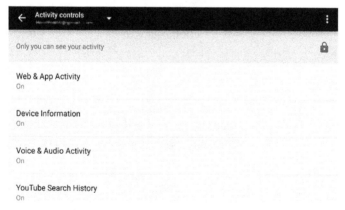

Select 'Activity & Privacy' and then 'Activity controls'. From here you can turn off different types of tracking activities and also delete any activities logged in the past.

Personal info and privacy

Choose 'Google' from the settings app to manage your privacy through a number of options, many of which are links to your Google account on the Internet. Tap 'Personal info & privacy' and then 'Your Personal info' to view and change your personal details that Google holds.

Chrome

To manage your privacy and options go to 'Menu' (three vertical dots in the app), choose 'Settings' and then 'Privacy'. From this menu you can turn on the browser's 'Do not track', 'clear cookies' and other data that has been collected and stored on the device in the cache.

Go back to 'Settings' and tap 'Site settings' to configure permissions such as location, camera and cookies site by site.

Apps

Each app you install on Android has its own settings and permission that cannot be generalised. It really is a case of going to the settings for each app and changing them accordingly.

Handset security

Set a passcode, passphrase, PIN or any other security mechanism that the phone manufacturer has provided to lock the handset. Also set a short time-out delay for the display. Review the options on your device, as you may be able to encrypt the data.

7.3 Antivirus

Antivirus applications for smartphones can be found through either the Apple Store for iOS devices or Google Play for Android. A number of providers of free antivirus for computers and laptops also provide antivirus for smartphones.

7.4 VPN

Another essential security requirement for smartphones is the VPN. Just like the VPN you might use for your home computer or laptop, this will encrypt the data connection between your smartphone and the destination server when using insecure public Wi-Fi. See section 6.3.

7.5 USB charging points

An increasing number of public locations offer USB charging points, particularly those with public waiting areas such as airports. It is highly improbable there is an inspection regime in place to make sure these have not been tampered with, so be extremely cautious when considering using one of these points to charge your devices. Malware could be embedded that could then be transferred to any device plugged into the charging point.

To avoid using a USB charging point, carry a cable and plug adaptor, or charge your USB devices using your laptop or a portable charging unit.

7.6 Bluetooth

Bluetooth can be very useful for exchanging information with other Bluetooth-enabled devices but it can also be a significant risk. Bluetooth is used to connect smartphones with other devices such as hands-free speakers and car audio systems.

The risk with Bluetooth is that when it is turned on it radiates an uncontrolled signal that any device in the area could connect with, so any device could have a means to access your phone without you knowing.

Best practice is to only turn Bluetooth on when you need to connect to a device, and make sure the device you connect to is the intended device. If you are unsure whether you have connected to the correct device, 'forget' the device and re-pair.

7.7 Mobile device disposal

When disposing of a laptop, tablet, smartphone or any other type of mobile device you want to make sure there is little or no chance of any of your information still being on it. This is the same whether the device is being traded second hand, passed to a friend or family member, or being destroyed.

For laptops that are being traded or passed on, reinstall the operating system over the original install; this is a rewrite and the best way to protect your information. Another way is to format the drive, just as you might for a computer.

For laptops that are being destroyed, remove the memory from the device, which is traditionally accessed by a little panel in the base, then physically destroy the memory.

Tablets and smartphones have a 'Reset' option to reset the device to the factory installation in the settings menu. This overwrites all your information, taking the device back to a clean state.

Tablets and smartphones might have a SIM or memory card inserted, in which case these should also be removed.

CHAPTER 8: CONSUMERS

Every person has rights as a consumer in what you buy or what service provider you use. Companies that provide these goods or services are always seeking to use technology and information to provide better services, improve their offering so that they can attract more customers, and improve efficiency to provide their goods or services at less expense.

Companies do this by collecting consumers' information and analysing it, but you have the right to expect these companies to protect your information and use it responsibly.

8.1 Certifications

Before trusting companies with your information you can research their record for data protection on the Internet. checking if they have been penalised for a data breach or seeing if they have a certificate for information security. Here are some certifications that companies may have and what they mean.

Although they display a commitment to information security, certifications are mainly for other businesses' information for when they are looking for partners or suppliers. Regardless of the actual reason for pursuing them, these certifications display a commitment to security.

Cyber Essentials

Cyber Essentials is a UK government-endorsed certification that is considered the benchmark in the UK commercial sector and is mandated in the UK for companies that provide certain services to the UK public sector. It is gaining international recognition as a foundation certification of cyber security. Cyber Essentials certification is awarded when an organisation passes an assessment against five key cyber security measures.

This is the logo that will be displayed on websites of companies that have achieved Cyber Essentials certification. You can also check the certification of companies online.

Cyber Essentials Plus

Cyber Essentials Plus provides customers with a greater degree of confidence than the Cyber Essentials because it involves technical testing of the network security. Certification is achieved when a company has had some penetration testing completed to identify any vulnerabilities and weaknesses, which must then be fixed before certification is granted.

This is the logo that companies certified to Cyber Essentials Plus can display.

ISO 27001

ISO 27001 certification states that an organisation has an information security management system (ISMS). The scope of the certification can be limited and the certification does not necessarily cover all services the company or organisation offer.

This logo will be displayed on websites of companies that have been awarded ISO 27001 status, although some certification bodies provide their own version of the crest. The crest will include 'ISO 27001 certified'. The company must also have the certificate available. Check the details of the certificate, even by asking the company, as it must be certified against ISO 27001:2013 for the certification to be valid, and will describe which parts of the company are certified.

Payment Card Industry Data Security Standard (PCI DSS)

The PCI DSS is specifically for organisations that are able to accept payment cards such as chip and PIN,  contactless, credit cards, debit cards, etc. Organisations that have achieved this certification should provide the greatest level of confidence to the customer with regard to their payment card information. This is supported by regular technical penetration testing of the network.

This is the logo that companies certified to the PCI DSS can display. The crest may differ slightly but will include 'PCI DSS compliant'.

Kitemark for Secure Digital Transactions

Awarded by the British Standards Institute, this certification is awarded after independent testing to show the  organisation has security controls to protect or guard the financial and/or personal information it is handling.

Checking certifications

The main way to check is on the company's website. It may be displayed on the 'About us' page or a 'Certifications' page.

Some certifications can be checked on a central website: Cyber Essentials can be checked on the website of the certification bodies and ISO 27001 can be checked on the websites of the certification companies.

Certifications do not guarantee that your information is secure but they do give greater confidence that your information will have some protection and the company is responsible and committed to information security.

8.2 Online purchasing

Companies that process purchases online have to comply with minimum standards agreed by the PCI Security Standards Council. One is the need for encryption, which means the data is changed in certain ways so that it couldn't be understood if it was read by a person who is not supposed to see it. There are two key things to look for when buying online: the application protocol that the website uses, which is displayed in the address bar, and the padlock that shows the site is secure. What you are looking for is the 'https://' before the website address, which means the website is using a secure protocol.

All the information for the security of the site is found in or beside the address bar. The padlock shows the site is secure and the https:// shows a secure protocol is being used.

Hovering the mouse cursor over the padlock shows the name of the certificate authority.

Next to the padlock is an 'i', which will allow you to see the information for the site. This information is verified by the digital certificate authority. There is an icon to view further information that will allow you to verify the site is secure.

As a consumer you can see the security information for the site, including whether you have saved passwords for the site and what encryption standard is being used. This site is using TLS 1.2, which is an acceptable type of encryption for a PCI DSS-certified site that can accept payments.

There are many websites that offer you the option of storing your card details when you make a purchase with them. It is advised not to save your card details online as this is creating two new avenues through which your card details can be compromised, on your browser and also on the website.

8.3 Chip and PIN cards

There have been a number of technological innovations in recent years to make payments and online transactions easier. As the use of technology increases, so does the number of risks. This has certainly been the case with chip and PIN cards.

There are two main outcomes of an attack on Chip and PIN cards: information can be taken from the card that will allow payments to be made with those card details, and payments can be processed without the cardholder knowing, even when the cardholder is still holding the card.

These are some of the different types of attacks:

- By getting hold of the card, the card details can be used to make online purchases, or the card can be 'cloned' (an exact duplicate is made) and used overseas where chip and PIN is not used.
- A 'card skimmer' can read and record the card information. This is mainly seen at ATMs, and can be used with 'shoulder-surfing' where PIN numbers are viewed and remembered.
- Stealing the card information from a site where the details have been stored.

- Intercepting a new card in the mail and using it for online transactions.
- Using stolen information to request a new card from the card issuer.

You can do the following to prevent these types of attack, or to reduce their impact:

✓ Cover your hand when you are entering your PIN into terminals.

✓ Don't let the terminal be removed from your vision.

✓ Request the terminal be passed to you instead of giving your card to the retailer.

✓ Regularly review your card statements to identify unknown or strange transactions.

✓ Carry your card in an inside pocket, front pocket, closed purse or closed handbag to prevent pickpocketing.

8.4 Contactless cards

Contactless cards are chip-and-PIN cards with extra functionality, but the points above remain valid.

Contactless cards are used to make payments without even putting the card into a machine. They work with 'near field communication': the terminal can read the card from a very short distance, which allows the transaction.

With this technology comes a number of new risks. The dominant risk when using contactless cards is that a transaction can take place without the cardholder even knowing. Criminals use card readers in confined areas, so even when cards are in handbags, wallets or purses, transactions can still be made.

A handheld card reader can be seen in the image above which was published in the Daily Telegraph. (*www.telegraph.co.uk/technology/2016/02/17/if-you-have-a-contactless-card-watch-out-for-this-scam*). This image was reportedly captured on the London Underground. The carriage is congested, so it is likely that the person with the card reader was able to process lots of unauthorised transactions without the cardholder's knowledge, each at £30.

To help prevent these attacks, or reduce their impact on you, you can use an RFID-blocking sleeve or an RFID-blocking wallet or purse. Confirm the RFID-blocking device works by testing it against a reader in a retail outlet, then verify this by making a payment with the same reader.

There can also be accidental transactions if you have more than one contactless card. Transactions have been charged to the wrong card when the wallet is presented to make a purchase, which could be an issue if a card issued by your employer is contactless and an unauthorised purchase is questioned by the company.

An RFID-blocking wallet or purse will prevent your contactless card being used unintentionally. The wallet to the right is produced by Secrid (*www.secrid.com*) and can protect up to six cards, as well as hold notes. As of  November 2017 Secrid has put a single price of €50 on its mini-wallet so there should be little variation throughout Europe, and it can be bought from the company online.

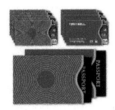 RFID-blocking sleeves can be bought through online marketplaces such as Amazon. The image to the left also shows RFID blocking passport sleeves. There have not been any reports of passports being read by this method, but as more countries are talking about developing digital passports with biometric information, sleeves such as these will be a good precaution.

8.5 Motioncard

An innovation that is being developed and trialled in mainland Europe is the Motioncard. When you make an online payment the details that are needed from your card are the long card number, the expiry date and the three-digit security code on the back of the card, known as the CVV.

The Motioncard has a digital CVV that changes every hour. It works with a payment system that records your card number and the CVV in use so that any payments you make can be authorised, but by changing the CVV every hour it means that if your card information is stolen, the card information will only be valid for up to an hour and will stop too many fraudulent purchases being made.

There is no indication when this technology will be available in the UK or Ireland.

8.6 Apple Pay and Internet of Things (IoT) payments

With the way technology and the IoT are developing, there are more devices that can be used to make payments. With an Apple Pay-enabled Apple Watch you can buy coffee with a flash of your wrist, or even a swipe of the phone if that has Apple Pay enabled.

A big risk with all these devices is that for you to use Apple Pay, they must have your card details saved on them. These devices are not as secure as computers or laptops because you cannot put as many security features on them. You should weigh up whether using Apple Pay on your watch or phone will be so convenient and make your life so much easier that it is worth the risk.

8.7 ATMs/Cashpoints

Automatic Teller Machine, or rather ATM, is the term used in the US for a cashpoint. It has also been used in the UK for cashpoints. For ease of reference ATM is used in this book.

There are two things an attacker needs to defraud a chip and PIN card: the card information and the PIN. Attackers will try many devious ways to get the card information and the PIN.

The common way to get the card information is by inserting a device inside the card reader that will copy the card details. These devices allow the intended transaction to be completed but will read the card information and store this so that a duplicate card can be created at a later time.

Alternatively, a false overlay could be fitted to the ATM, again with the intent of copying the card information. This is called card skimming. Once the information is copied from the card it could be cloned or the information could be used in any other way for the attacker's benefit at the victim's expense.

There are three things you can do to protect yourself when using ATMs:

- ✓ Check the ATM for any tampering, look for anything that you would not expect, or feel the individual components of the ATM to check they are secure and appear to be the device components.
- ✓ Be aware of the environment, particularly of people paying attention when you are entering the PIN.
- ✓ Use an ATM that is monitored within a secure area, for example in a bank lobby or in a retail outlet.

The following image was issued by the US FBI to explain what card skimming is.

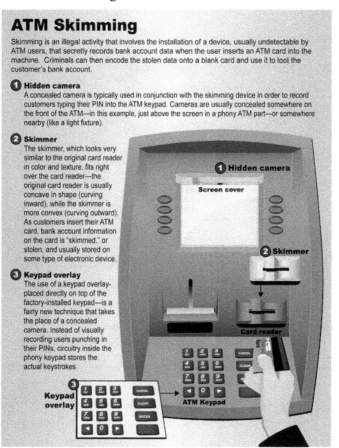

This following image is an illustration from Pakwired.com that shows how attackers use cashpoint machines against you.

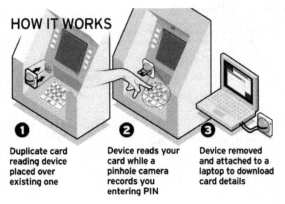

HOW IT WORKS

❶ Duplicate card reading device placed over existing one

❷ Device reads your card while a pinhole camera records you entering PIN

❸ Device removed and attached to a laptop to download card details

Seven tips to help you protect yourself from ATM theft:

1. Get in the habit of using the same ATM for your transactions. Become familiar with it and be able to recognise changes to the machine.
2. Use ATMs inside banks rather than on the street.
3. If you're visiting an unfamiliar ATM that is not inside a bank, examine it for devices. Card- or cash-trapping devices need to be glued or taped to the card reader or cash dispenser. Look for 'extra' cameras beyond the basic and generally obvious ATM security camera.
4. Never rely on the help of strangers to retrieve a card that is trapped in the ATM
5. Never use an ATM when other people are lingering.

6. Report cards trapped in the machine immediately. Try not to leave the machine. Call the bank from the ATM where your card was taken using a mobile phone, if at all possible.
7. Don't use ATMs with extra signage or warnings posted on the machine, these signs may be put there to divert your attention when you use the machine.

CHAPTER 9: PERSONAL AND CONSUMER RIGHTS

As a commercial user of services – a customer – you have a number of rights and expectations. The expectations are that commercial providers and businesses acknowledge their responsibilities, their duty of care, to protect your information that they hold in order to better serve you.

9.1 Personal information and your rights

As an individual you have the right for your information to be protected. The need for this has become significant since it was realised how much damage can be done, and how much crime can be committed, by malicious people when they get hold of personal information.

Data Protection Directive (DPD)

The DPD is European legislation that organisations, businesses and governments must comply with when using personal information. The Data Protection Principles are strict rules in the Directive that must be complied with. The eight principles are that personal information must be:

- ✓ Used fairly and lawfully;
- ✓ Used for limited, specifically stated purposes;
- ✓ Used in a way that is adequate, relevant and not excessive;
- ✓ Accurate;
- ✓ Kept for no longer than is absolutely necessary;

✓ Handled according to people's data protection rights;
✓ Kept safe and secure; and
✓ Not transferred outside the European Economic Area without adequate protection.

There is also stronger legal protection for more sensitive information, such as:

✓ Ethnic background;
✓ Political opinions;
✓ Religious beliefs;
✓ Health;
✓ Sexual health; and
✓ Criminal records.

There was an agreement between the European Union and the US called Safe Harbor, which provided a method for the 'safe' transfer of information between these territories, but this agreement collapsed when Max Schrems successfully challenged the agreement in the European courts in 2015. This focus on privacy rights began following the Edward Snowden revelations about US surveillance in 2013.

In 2016, Safe Harbor was replaced by an agreement called Privacy Shield. As stated on *www.privacyshield.gov*: "The EU-U.S. and Swiss-U.S. Privacy Shield Frameworks were designed by the U.S. Department of Commerce and the European Commission and Swiss Administration to provide companies on both sides of the Atlantic with a mechanism to comply with data protection requirements when transferring personal data from the European Union and Switzerland to the United States in support of transatlantic commerce."

The General Data Protection Regulation (GDPR)

The GDPR comes into effect on 25 May 2018 and supersedes the DPD and any laws based on the DPD.

The GDPR has a core set of principles for how information is managed. The information must be:

- ✓ Processed lawfully, fairly and in a transparent manner in relation to individuals;
- ✓ Collected for specified, explicit and legitimate purposes and not further processed in a manner that is incompatible with those purposes;
- ✓ Adequate, relevant and limited to what is necessary in relation to the purposes for which they are processed;
- ✓ Accurate and, where necessary, kept up to date;
- ✓ Kept in a form which permits identification of data subjects for no longer than is necessary for the purposes for which the personal data are processed; and
- ✓ Processed in a manner that ensures appropriate security of the personal data, including protection against unauthorised or unlawful processing and against accidental loss, destruction or damage, using appropriate technical or organisational measures.

The GDPR addresses the transfer of information overseas in separate articles.

A big difference with the GDPR is accountability. Organisations must show how they comply with the requirements, e.g. the recording of decisions on the processing of information.

The GDPR also includes a number of rights for individuals:

- ✓ The right to be informed.
- ✓ The right of access.
- ✓ The right to rectification.
- ✓ The right to erasure – commonly referred to as the right to be forgotten.
- ✓ The right to restrict processing.
- ✓ The right to data portability.
- ✓ The right to object.
- ✓ Rights in relation to automated decision making and profiling.

There is also a requirement for certain organisations to have a data protection officer, and requirements for handling subject access requests. Subject access requests can be used to get a copy of information that a company holds about you. From the time the request is received, the company or organisation has a maximum of 30 days to respond.

An additional requirement is to present a breach notification if a company is breached.

Another significant change with the GDPR is the potential penalties for non-compliance: up to 4% of a company's annual global turnover or €20,000,000.

The GDPR is overseen, including how subject access requests are managed and responded to, by the national supervisory body. This is the Data Protection Commissioner in Ireland and the Information Commissioner's Office (ICO) in the UK.

NIS Directive

The GDPR is supported by two other pieces of legislation, the first of which is the NIS Directive. All European member states must make national legislation that complies with the Directive. This national legislation is due to come into force at the same time as the GDPR, in May 2018.

The Directive is more for governments and communication providers than anyone else, so Internet providers, Cloud marketplace providers and search engines must also comply. The aim of the Directive is to foster more communication between European member states, create national cyber security organisations and make these organisations more 'open' in the way they operate, particularly if they suffer a breach of their network – all to manage the security and stability of Europe's critical infrastructure and to protect as many Internet users as possible.

ePrivacy Regulation

The ePrivacy Directive 2002 is due to be replaced in 2018. Although there has not been much reported about the new regulation, they will change the security responsibilities for a number of online communications providers that were not subject to such regulations in Europe before. The new regulation covers organisations such as Facebook, Twitter and Instagram.

There are a number of key elements of the ePrivacy Regulation:

- Privacy of both content and metadata is covered. Content is what you say in the message, the picture you send, the text and/or even the video you send. The metadata is all the contextual information, such as the location it was sent from, the source of the communication, and the time, date and length of the communication. Communication providers must now delete the metadata, unless you give consent for it to be used for certain purposes, such as stopping communication services being used for fraud. It is likely there will be new agreements issued by all online communication providers during or leading up to May 2018, which will include a request for this consent.
- Your communication cannot be intercepted and read by anyone unless there is a national law that allows it and only for a specific genuine purpose, e.g. to stop terrorism or criminal activities.
- All communication providers must get your consent in the first place and also renew that consent every six months.
- The consent needed for cookies is managed. If the cookies are only getting certain types of information, the organisation does not need to get consent, but you

must also be able to manage cookies in your browser settings.

- Changes to direct marketing include:
  - o Unsolicited direct marketing is not allowed. This means companies can no longer send marketing communications, emails, texts, etc. without controlling who they are sending it to.
  - o You must give consent for organisations to send you direct marketing communications, and you must be able to opt out of the marketing communications in the future if you change your mind.
  - o Telephone marketing callers must show their number when calling or use a special prefix to their number that shows it is a marketing call. They cannot hide their number.
- Organisations that do not comply with the Regulation can be fined up to €20,000,000 or 4% of their previous year's global turnover, in line with GDPR penalties.
- People whose information is compromised due to a breach can seek compensation from the provider. This is mainly when the communication provider did not do enough to protect your information.

9.2 Reviewing a company

As a consumer you often have freedom of choice as to which provider you use for services. If using a service will involve them having your personal information, you could check to see whether they have had information or cyber security failings, which would indicate their commitment to protecting their information and the information of their clients. There are a number of ways to do this, including a search on the Internet or checking specific sites such as data protection authorities. There is a data protection authority in each territory in Europe. A full list of the European Commission National Data Protection Authorities is available at *http://ec.europa.eu/justice/data-protection/bodies/authorities/index_en.htm.*

In the UK the authority is the ICO at *www.ico.org.uk*. The UK government has declared that it will implement the GDPR. The UK government has demonstrated that it intends to abide by the GDPR post-Brexit by presenting the Data Protection Bill 2017, which will enshrine all of the requirements of the GDPR in British law.

In Ireland the authority is the Data Protection Commissioner at *www.dataprotection.ie*.

9.3 Medical information and institutions

Attackers have realised that private healthcare information is also an easy way to get your financial information, or to get enough of your personal information to steal your identity. Private medical records, such as in the US or Ireland, often contain financial information and they also tend to have a lot of lifestyle and contact information, which could be used for profiling you.

Medical institutions tend to prioritise the availability of your information at the expense of its security, although they are being held to account after some significant and highly publicised failures, such as the major data breaches at medical institutions in the US, as well as recent ransomware attacks in UK and Ireland.

9.4 Plans and activities

Another significant type of information that attackers would like to get about you is any plans you have made, as these can reveal times when you will be especially vulnerable, such as when you will be away from home (to potentially rob your house), when you are going on holiday and where you are travelling from (in which case your car could be parked in long-term parking and could be stolen).

Attackers will look for single bits of information that will reveal this, including from your or your children's social networking sites, or they will take many snippets of information that together will reveal a planned activity.

Other things attackers will look for is information that could help them conduct an attack, such as birthdays, favourite pets and nicknames – all of which tend to be used as passwords. They will also look for pictures inside your house, codes for security systems in the house, where security systems are located in the home, and so on – all of which will help them attack your house in less time, reducing the chance of them getting caught.

9.5 Big data

Where attackers might get all information that is available online about you to target you, companies continually gather information about their users and consumers' habits online to identify trends and develop marketing. The information these companies capture and use to profile their customers is called 'big data'. Big data is about the analysis of the information, not so much about the volume of information.

Big data analysis takes massive sets of data to identify trends, patterns, habits and any other type of output that could be used to improve the company's marketing, development, or even popularity or reputation.

CHAPTER 10: INTERNET OF THINGS (IOT)

IoT describes all devices that can connect to the Internet.

Table 5: IoT devices

Fridge	Kettle	Toaster	Doorbell	Car
Fish tank	Walking stick	Home CCTV system	Internal IP camera	Digital SLR camera
Fitness tracker	Television	Hairbrush	Oven	Mirror
Air purifier	Home heating system	Garden sprinkler system	Dog collar	Slippers
Breathalyser	Shoes	T-shirt	Coffee machine	Toothbrush
Vending machine	Christmas tree	Parking meter	Baby monitor	Pacemaker

IoT devices can present a significant number of security risks because manufacturers are trying to get the technology onto the market in the quickest time possible to be the leading product, but usually at the expense of security. Devices could present far fewer security risks if more time was spent developing their security features.

There are some things that can be done to manage the potential risks when joining IoT devices to home networks.

10.1 Default password

Any device that is built for the IoT will have to connect to your network, which will be managed in the configuration that is protected by a password. When the device is released from the manufacturer it will either have no password or a default password taken from a list that is common among all the same devices. The first requirement for any IoT device (or any password-protected device at all) should be to change the default password. Guidance on creating and managing passwords and passphrases is included in section 5.1.

10.2 Firewall

Firewalls can secure home networks and IoT devices, but there are no free IoT firewalls available at the time of writing.

F-Secure SENSE

The SENSE adds a layer of security to your home network. It connects to your home router and scans your network. SENSE connects to F-Secure's Secure Cloud, which is a large library of known viruses and threats. If the device notices suspicious activity or identifies a virus or threat that is in the library, it sends an alert to the controlling device. SENSE can be installed on smartphones, tablets and computers, and these devices are where the alerts are sent to. SENSE is available at *www.f-secure.com*.

Luma Wi-Fi router

The manufacturer says this device "will bring enterprise-level security to your home". It uses intrusion and virus detection to monitor traffic for malware-like behaviour, suspicious activity and quarantine infected devices. The router is available at *www.lumahome.com*.

This device has not had the most positive reviews and also appears to be expensive in comparison with other devices.

Dojo

Dojo-Labs has designed an extremely easy-to-use device that connects to your router using an Ethernet cable. Dojo acts as the home network gatekeeper. The device monitors all incoming and outgoing traffic, has a perusal and analysis function, and profiles network devices at configuration. If the device identifies abnormal behaviour or an issue, it sends an alert to the app, which is designed like messaging apps. The device also has a 'glowing-rock gadget', which is designed to be moved around the home so that it is visible. The glowing-rock reports the level of security of the home network by glowing green, orange or red. The device is available at *www.dojo-labs.com*.

Cujo

Cujo has an easy-to-use interface and a combination of antivirus, firewall, malware and deep packet-inspection technology. Cujo is a Cloud-connected device that was funded by crowdfunding. Cujo looks like a coffee mug, activates itself when it is plugged into an empty socket on the router and requires no further setup. It is managed through an easy-to-use app. There is a subscription fee that can be paid monthly or annually. Cujo is available at *www.getcujo.com*.

10.3 Network vulnerability management

Network vulnerability management sounds very technical but it is not. It involves getting a network vulnerability scanner and using it to look at the home network. The scanner will identify vulnerabilities, which usually results in installing patches or updates that have not been automatically installed.

There are many vulnerability management providers that allow for a number of free scans of a network. Some providers will allow up to ten free network scans. It can be fairly straightforward to start a vulnerability scan on a home network, and the results are very easy to understand. Any vulnerability discovered could be a problem, so follow the guidance of the vulnerability management scanner to fix the problem.

Ideally a vulnerability management scan would be done every month, on the same date each month.

10.4 Disposal of IoT devices

One thing about IoT that is not normally covered is how to replace a device without giving away your information. A person buying a second-hand IoT device could get a lot more than they bargained for if any of your personal information or secret information is on it, which they could sell or even use against you. Attackers might even buy used devices just to see if there is any information left on them.

On most IoT devices there will be a way to reset the device to factory settings. On many smaller devices the reset button is a pin button: a button that is flush to the case of the device that needs a pin to be pushed.

If the IoT device does not have a reset button, remove and destroy the hard drive. The hard drive is the part that stores any secret or personal information.

Once the hard drive has been removed, take the device to the recycling depot where it can be disposed of according to relevant local laws and European regulations.

10.5 Cyber physical security

Cyber physical security systems are security devices that can connect to the network that manages physical security, e.g. CCTV systems, internal IP cameras and volumetric alarm systems. Home users are generally daunted by these technologies and will rely on security professionals to install them.

Reputable registered security professionals should be engaged to install these devices. Ask the installer how to change the default password.

As with the risk posed by connecting IoT devices to the network, you are possibly revealing information about you or your habits that could be useful for an attacker. It may only be a small piece of information, a single habit or a single regular thing you do, but many small pieces of information, habits or regularly repeated activities could be put together to make a bigger picture that an attacker could use against you.

Before you add any IoT device to your home, ask:

☑ Is the benefit of the device worth the risk?

☑ What do you need to do to manage the risk, such as the default password or where the device is placed in the home?

☑ Who can access the information on or from the device?

☑ Who can change the settings on the device?

CHAPTER 11: SOCIAL NETWORKING SECURITY

Every social networking application has security settings that must be assessed before being applied.

You need to be aware of your whole internet and social networking profile. While you initially created the profile, your friend's posts may also be part of that profile. It is your profile to manage, ask for posts to be taken down if needed.

11.1 Facebook

There are a number of security features in Facebook that allow you to keep access to your account secure, but this is only one aspect of your security. Other things to consider include how much of your profile is visible to other users who are not your friends, and how public any posts or photos are.

'Settings' is located on your Facebook homepage from a drop-down as seen below.

When you enter 'Settings', 'Security and login' is the second item in the left-hand column. There are a number of elements to 'Security and login'.

'Recommended'

'Choose friends to contact if you are locked out' – "these are friends you chose who can securely help if you ever have trouble accessing your account". Your 'trusted' contacts are given codes that they can give to you if ever you need help to access your account.

'Where you're logged in' – this displays all devices that you are logged in to your account with, so this is a good place to check that your account is only being accessed from devices you own. Check the devices that are listed, make sure they are your devices and that the location or area for each device is correct.

'Login'

'Change password' – use a complex password or, even better, a passphrase to access your account. Complex passwords and passphrases are explained in section 5.1.

11.2 LinkedIn

LinkedIn is a professional networking site. It is primarily financed by advertising and also premium membership subscriptions. It is a worldwide network with professionals from every nation registered and active online, whether that is in groups or in the wider LinkedIn community. LinkedIn has many products within its profile, including jobs, groups, learning and business services. LinkedIn users want to be acknowledged for their professional role or status, especially when it comes to having other professionals endorse their professional skills and knowledge.

Security on LinkedIn is very much oriented around the communications you receive.

11.3 Plenty of Fish

Plenty of Fish is a dating site. It is highly probable there are people on this site who are using false profiles, also known as catfishing. If you are interested in a profile in this application, view other social networking sites or search engines to see what information is available about the person.

11.4 Tinder

Tinder is an app for those seeking physical relationships. It has become synonymous with the left swipe to like and right swipe to reject. It is also likely that catfishing occurs on this application, so check profiles on other sites and through searches.

11.5 WhatsApp

WhatsApp uses encryption keys to verify users. You can turn on notifications so that you are informed if these keys change. If a key is changed, you could accidentally message an impersonator instead of your contact. Share this guidance so your contacts will also get the notifications.

If you get a notification, verify with your contact through another type of communication, such as by phone or email. The only real reason there should be a key change is if they have changed handsets.

It is a very simple process to turn on the WhatsApp 'Security Settings & Notifications'.

1. Go to 'Settings' (on iPhones this is bottom-right of the main menu screen in the app; on Android devices click the three vertical dots menu from the app's main menu).
2. Tap 'Account'.
3. Tap 'Security'.
4. Turn on 'Show Security Notifications'.

11.6 Snapchat

The misconception with most Snapchat users is that their image is only live for a few seconds before being deleted, which is invariably not the case. Personalise the security settings for your security and privacy.

There are certain quirks or features of Snapchat that should be understood before you use them.

Snapchat thread

A thread in Snapchat is the number of messages between users in a conversation. With Snapchat, users can be rated by the length of the thread and how often it is read or replied to.

A user's thread will go down in the rankings, or rather popularity, if there is no activity in the thread for five minutes. This could make some people be on their account all the time in order to stay up in the popularity ratings.

Snapchat Maps

Snapchat Maps is also referred to as 'Snapchat ghost' or 'friend-stalking'. This feature allows you to see exactly where your friends are, what they are doing and even if they are standing up.

There are a significant number of risks if this feature were compromised because of the level of information it would reveal about you, your activities, your family and your friends. This is a new app and the vulnerabilities have not been bought to light yet.

The feature is managed in the location features. Select 'Ghost mode' to turn off the location tagging.

Securing Snapchat

Here are the top ten tips to improve your Snapchat security:

1. Turn on login verification – go to the 'Camera' tab, tap the ghost icon (top middle of screen), tap the gear icon (top right) and go to the 'Login Verification' option.

2. Restrict who can contact you – go to the 'Camera' tab, tap the ghost icon (top middle of screen), go to 'Who can... Contact Me' and set it to 'My Friends'.

3. Restrict who can see your stories – go to the 'Camera' tab, tap the ghost icon (top middle of screen), go to 'Who can... View My Story' and select 'My Friends or Custom' (to build a list).

4. Hide yourself from 'Quick Add' – go to the 'Camera' tab, tap the ghost icon (top middle of screen) and if it is enabled select 'See Me in Quick Add' to turn it off.

5. Review random users who add you – go to the 'Profile' tab, tap 'Added Me' and choose whether to block or ignore.

6. Screenshot notifications – turn on the notifications for the Snapchat app in your device settings. This will notify you as instant phone notifications as well as in the app, so you will see the notifications even if you have closed the app.

7. Snapcode and username management – don't share a screenshot of your snapcode anywhere online as random users may add you as a friend. Don't share your username if you want to keep your activity and interactions more intimate.

8. Use 'My eyes only' – you can move 'Memories' images to 'My eyes only' to prevent others seeing these images. Tap the checkmark option in the top-right corner of 'Memories', select the images you want to make 'My eyes only' and tap the lock icon at the bottom of the screen.

9. Check destination – get into the habit of double-checking who you are sending snaps to. If you are replying to a snap, tap their username at the bottom and select who you do or do not want to be included.

10. Learn to delete – if you need to delete a story that you may regret having posted, go to your 'Stories' tab, tap your story that you want to delete, swipe up and touch the trash can icon at the top to delete the story. You have to repeat the process for each story.

11.7 Twitter

Tweeting on Twitter has almost continuously grown in popularity. There are some things you can do to protect the security of your tweets and your privacy.

Security and privacy settings

Go to *www.twitter.com*, click the gear icon, choose 'Settings' and select 'Security and privacy'.

Access

Login verification is the first setting, which is set to off by default. You can increase security by enabling a send verification option, either to your phone by text or the Twitter mobile app.

Password reset

By default this is set to off. Enable 'Require personal information to reset my password'.

Photo tagging

Set by default to allow anyone to tag you in photos; change this to either people you follow or do not allow anyone to tag you in photos.

Tweet privacy

By default this is off. If you check the box to protect your Tweets, this locks down your visibility a lot, but it also severely restricts what can be done with your tweets, i.e. they cannot be retweeted, etc.

Tweet location

By default this is off; it is best to leave it off.

Discoverability

This is on by default, which allows people to find you by your email address, whether they know your Twitter handle or not. It is better to turn it off.

Personalisation

Turn it off by unchecking the box next to 'Tailor Twitter based on my recent website visits'.

Promoted content

Turn off 'Tailor ads based on information shared by ad partners' by unchecking the box.

Review

Occasionally the options and settings in Twitter are updated, which can affect your selections. Visit the Security and Privacy settings every so often to see if anything has changed.

CHAPTER 12: PARENTAL SECURITY

As well as preparing their children for possible threats they might face outside the home, parents must also prepare their children for threats they might encounter in the home, particularly online.

A very difficult message for children to learn is that threats might exist on the internet, a resource that is full of so much information and adds so much value to their lives, as well as letting them chat to their friends and play games online.

12.1 Managing online security for children

DLC, GTA, Robox, Minecraft, Avatar – these are all terms in children's language that have evolved along with the technology and its use. Coding and computer science are in curriculums, and children are growing up with technology.

The one aspect that children tend to be unaware of is the threats that exist on the Internet. There is an indication that older children are more tolerant of breaches and accept they will be hacked and children in general are often less concerned about managing their security effectively.

Top ten messages for children

1. Once it is on the Internet it stays on the Internet.

2. You say it, you own it.

3. What you say now will impact your future.

4. Anyone can post on the Internet, so it should be checked before being believed.

5. Anyone can be who they want on the Internet, so be cautious of profiles.

6. Talk about it, don't hide it.

7. Think twice, click once.

8. Read your post before you post. What does it say to you?

9. Check profiles of friends, check elsewhere and then check again.

10. Search yourself occasionally – it is amazing what you might discover.

12.2 Threats to children

Cyber bullying

Cyber bullying is a serious issue as the victims cannot seek security or protection in their own home. The Internet means if there is bullying, it is constant and can reach into places where children feel safest: the home, their bedroom, their sanctuary.

Cyber bullying is bullying that takes place using electronic means. Cyber bullying is using technology to harass, threaten, target or embarrass another person. The bullying can occur over social networks, mobile phones, emails, texts or any other type of electronic communication.

Cyber bullying is a significant threat to children of all ages because contact with the bullies is potentially relentless. The most common means for cyber bullying is the mobile phone. Social networks – which are also accessed via mobile phone – are also a significant platform for cyber bullying.

For parents, the main way to manage the threat of cyber bullying is communication: talking with children, discussing what cyber bullying is, discussing what it could look like and discussing what to do if there is any suggestion that children are experiencing cyber bullying.

Grooming

Grooming is not an activity or a threat that should be taken lightly. There are many agencies and national authorities that have dedicated internet sites and resources for grooming, such as Barnardos, ISPCC, NSPCC and Childline. If there is any concern that grooming is taking place the first thing to do is refer to one of these resources.

Grooming takes a long time to achieve and can be very difficult to understand, unless you have been a victim. The brief I received from a social work professional and also Police experts gave me a basic understanding of the threat.

Grooming is when someone takes the time and makes the effort to befriend someone so they can gain the person's trust and get them to do things that are wrong or not nice.

If the child is old enough parents could deliver this message using terms such as sexual abuse, sexual exploitation or trafficking. If the child is younger the message could be relayed using characters the child can relate to, such as

Spiderman or Peppa Pig. The whole purpose of the message is to let the child know there is a risk and to encourage the child to communicate.

Grooming will start with small gestures then gradually increase until the child is entrapped. The gestures will not necessarily increase in 'size' but will involve acts by the child that could be considered greater abuses of their trust, or rather acts that are more serious as they continue.

Grooming is not limited to the Internet or even to strangers. Grooming can be face to face or online, or by a professional, a person in a position of trust, a stranger, a family friend or even a family member. Grooming can start in many ways: friending on social networking sites, in-game friending, or even making the first meeting at a playground, park or any other area where children group.

Grooming occurs through a process of escalation. The person doing the grooming will get the child to do something that they would need to keep from their parents, which helps build a bond of trust with the child. As the bond of trust escalates, the child will potentially become withdrawn from their parents and will isolate themselves in the family home.

A potential progression or escalation could start from a person giving a child an ice cream to initiate the relationship, which could then progress as follows: drinking Coke, eating chewing gum, going home late, going places they are not supposed to go to, using bad language, smoking, drinking, stealing from the home, shoplifting or even further than that.

The person doing the grooming will lower the inhibitions of the child. There is a big market for child pornography and the groomer will try to use the child for some sexual purpose, either for their own gratification or to sell to the illegal market.

Trust, honesty and communication between parent and child will help prevent grooming. There is no guaranteed formula to prevent a child being groomed, but the main message is to encourage open and honest communication.

There is no stereotype for a groomer: they can be any age, male or female, any ethnicity and work in any profession.

Many children and young people don't understand that they have been groomed or that what has happened is abuse.

There are three key messages for parents or responsible adults:

1. Use examples, scenarios or 'actors' that the children can relate to: superheroes, pop stars, cartoon characters, television characters.
2. Use language and words that children can understand. Avoid difficult words and don't use words such as 'exploitation' – this would be better phrased as 'take advantage of' or 'use for a bad purpose'.
3. Avoid being condescending. Don't talk down to the children with your use of words, also lower your body so you are talking to them face to face.

Friending

'Friending' means making friends, but online friends are not the same as friends made in traditional ways. Accumulating friends is sometimes regarded as an achievement in today's society, with some people using their number of friends as a measure of status.

The Internet provides a mask for predators to hide behind, so they will pretend to be someone else in order to friend children, who they could then possibly manipulate and even groom.

Blue Whale Challenge

The Blue Whale Challenge game was reportedly first seen in Russia. It is an online game that requires participants to complete 50 challenges. Reportedly the challenges are set by an online administrator and could involve self-harm, watching horror films and waking at unusual hours.

Apparently the final challenge is suicide. Although the game has not been directly linked to children suicides it is reported that there have been over 130 suicides in Russia within a certain period and all the children appeared to visit common social networking sites. The participants join an online community that goads and encourages them to complete the challenges.

Parents can only talk to children about peer pressure, applying their own choices and saying no to peer pressure. It would be worthwhile speaking to children about the game before they encounter the game.

The Blue Whale Challenge is a trend, which as with any other trend will fade away. When the trend of this game fades it will probably be replaced by another trend, which could be just as dangerous or even more so.

News of trends is shared using social media, so parents might want to look at social media to see what current trends are or what may be developing. Another option is getting the child to be the parents' eyes on the Internet to inform them of what is happening. Children might be more responsive to this task as it recognises their maturity and also gives them a security responsibility in the home.

12.3 Inappropriate content

Inappropriate content is a general term for information such as:

1. Images that might upset your child.
2. Material that is directed at adults.
3. Information – accurate or inaccurate – that might tempt or lead your child into unlawful or dangerous behaviour.
4. Visual depictions (images) that are obscene.
5. Child pornography.

Only a parent can truly decide what is inappropriate content for their children as only they know their children's maturity.

Parents can manage access to many aspects of inappropriate content by using parental controls.

The main way parents can work with their children to manage the impact of inappropriate content is to talk to them, discuss what inappropriate content is, discuss what the children should do if they happen upon inappropriate content, and discuss how the children should talk about this with their parents.

Sexting

Sexting is covered in 'The how – threats' section. Sexting is a significant threat to children who may not understand or appreciate what the activity could lead to.

Sextortion

Sextortion is using sexual content to extort a child or other vulnerable person. Sexting is potentially the first step that could lead to sextortion. If a person has exchanged sexual content with someone, the second person could threaten to release or share the content unless the first person does something. With sextortion the required action could involve some kind of sexual act or activity.

12.4 Protect and manage

Parents want to protect their children and support them in their development while managing the exposure of their children to anything negative or that may affect them.

There are two aims for parents in sharing security education and awareness with their children:

- Protect: Develop the mindset: that of suspicion and caution.
- Manage: Deliver the in-home support, security education and awareness in an age-appropriate manner to develop their children's understanding.

Parents should aim to support children in understanding these aspects, and encourage questions and discussions about risks and threats on the Internet and in the digital world.

Suspicion and caution

Not everybody on the Internet is who they say they are, nor is all the information on the Internet accurate or true. There are many stories of false profiles being used to lure children or engage them, pretending to be a professional, a peer or someone else they could relate to.

This will be a very hard message to get children to listen to, but there are numerous resources dedicated to this that you should explore with your children.

Reference sites such as Wikipedia are compiled by random users. There is no authority regulating these sites, so any information can be uploaded with absolutely no guarantee that it is accurate.

Encourage the use of more than one site to confirm information on the Internet, especially when accuracy is required, such as for homework.

Appropriate delivery

Appropriate delivery breaks down into relevance and style.

Relevance

There is no benefit trying to educate a person on iPhone security if they only use Android devices, or educating a person on threats to home users when they only use tablets.

Style

There is no benefit trying to educate a six-year-old by using words such as 'malicious', 'exploitation', 'nefarious'. These words will mean nothing to them and the purpose or value of the education will be ignored and lost. When speaking to the youngest group of children it is essential that age-appropriate content and style are used. When explaining any issues to the younger of the groups relate the lesson to characters they will identify with, such as Peppa Pig, Paw Patrol, Jake and the Neverland Pirates, Scooby-Doo, The Flash, Superman or Teenage Mutant Ninja Turtles.

There is no benefit trying to educate a teenager using Peppa Pig or Paw Patrol. When explaining the need to secure personal storage and profiles, an example such as the iCloud hack of celebrities' personal profiles should be used for teenagers, who can relate to celebrities such as Jennifer Lawrence, Kaley Cuoco and Kate Upton. With teenagers it is essential to consider the gender of the example. There is a high probability that both male and female teenagers will identify with three celebrities mentioned above as girls want to follow their style, make-up tips, etc. and boys find them attractive.

There are also lots of reports of celebrities having their personal information, such as private photos, 'hacked' and released online. Use examples of this reporting to highlight the need to protect their online profile and information.

Communication

Communication is key. Regularly discuss the Internet with your child, be interested in what they are saying and stop it becoming a taboo topic. Be interested in what they have discovered and explore the benefits, but use the conversation to encourage them to realise that risks exist.

The key aspect of communication is context: not referring to technology but using characters who children can relate to as mentioned earlier.

Children will be talking with their friends about the common technologies, and they will be using and learning about technology at school. They will marvel at what can be achieved and will want to share this learning. To them, this knowledge is new, so marvel at their learning.

Share aware

Talk to your children about unwanted advances, how these will appear and why it would benefit them to share this with you. Discuss these things so that they become common topics.

Mistakes will happen

Discuss mistakes. Don't chastise but discuss why they are mistakes and how to avoid them, and praise their honesty and maturity for admitting the mistake.

Don't deny the Internet – if you do it might bury the technology and increase the risk

Avoid denying the Internet as a punishment for a mistake. If that is the threat, children will tend to find a way to access the Internet but not discuss anything they encounter, good or bad.

Teach through responsibility

Give them a responsibility, such as searching the names of family members monthly. This means they learn about how information can be discovered online and gives them a responsible task that they can own.

What they say online stays online

This is one of the life lessons that they will need to be introduced to, but conceptually it will be very difficult to get them to understand or appreciate the potential impact. The easiest way to get the message across will be to use characters.

It will be difficult for children to understand that an action today will affect them tomorrow. Social network profiling is becoming a practice within the recruitment process for some organisations. What children post online today can affect their future.

They say it, they own it

Another aspect that children will have difficulty understanding is that if they post something online, it will remain accountable to them and could affect them in the future.

Search their name online, regularly

Regularly search the names of your children online. Use the results to demonstrate earlier points such as 'they say it, they own it' and 'what they say online stays online'.

Another option is to set up a Google Alert, which will send you an email whenever their name appears on the Internet. See section 3.2 for more information on this.

Their era, their technology, their world

Children have coding and computer science in their curriculum at school, so as far as they are concerned this technology is their era. They might well believe they know more about technology than you, so encourage them and let them teach you things that will totally enthuse them.

Homepage

Set the homepage and screen saver of the home computer so that there is an acceptable image or even a message on the screen.

Consistency

If you entrust the care of your children to a responsible adult, discuss the Internet rules that are used at home so that there is consistency in the management of their Internet use.

Think twice, click once

This is a very important message: encourage children to think about what they are doing before they commit.

Charging station

Discourage taking mobile phones and/or mobile devices into the bedroom. Establish a house charging point. Make sure there are fire prevention measures for the charging station.

Desktop location

Set the desktop computer in a location where it can be viewed by everybody. Sneak a peek every now and then, just for peace of mind.

Accounts

Create accounts for each user, keeping the administrator account for the control of the system. The administrator should have their own account so that they are 'treated' the same as everyone else.

Parental controls

There are ways to set parental controls on all devices:

Windows: use the following link or search 'parental controls': *https://support.microsoft.com/en-us/help/12416/microsoft-account-family-settings*.

Or you can set up a family account. Go to account.microsoft.com/family.

Apple devices: *https://support.apple.com/en-us/HT201813*.

Google Safety Centre:
www.google.ie/safetycenter/families/start/#control-what-your-family-sees-on-the-web.

Time limits

Set time limits for use, and a cut-off time for using devices.

Open doors

Have an agreement in place that bedroom doors are left open when mobile devices are used in bedrooms.

Alarm clock

Buy alarm clocks for bedrooms so that there is no need to take mobile phones into bedrooms.

CHAPTER 13: RESILIENCE

Resilience is all about having the ability to 'recover from a disruption'. A disruption can be anything from the loss of power to the loss of a system; anything that could interfere with your ability to use your technology as intended.

The main thing you can do for resilience is make sure you have your data backed up on a device that is not permanently attached to your computer. That way, if there is any type of malware that gets onto your computer, it doesn't also affect your backup device. It is fairly easy to restore a computer to how it was when it was bought new, but it is nearly impossible to recover your information.

When you are using devices for backup these are the main things to do:

☑ Format the device to remove any software that is not required.

☑ Install encryption so that all information is encrypted.

☑ Use a good passphrase to restrict access.

☑ Use a date when creating a backup so that you can easily see which is the latest backup;

☑ Ideally use more than one backup device by rotation so that you are not dependent on one device, i.e. use backup device one in odd weeks, and use backup device two for even weeks.

☑ Store the two backup devices separately so that if the backup storage location is attacked, both backup devices will not be stolen at the same time.

☑ Store one backup device away from the home so that if the computer is stolen or destroyed, there is a much smaller chance that the backup will also be stolen or destroyed.

☑ Consider a secure location for the alternative backup, such as a safety deposit box.

CHAPTER 14: PERSONAL CYBER SECURITY RISK ASSESSMENT

A risk assessment is a tool that is frequently used by businesses to show where risks might exist to their systems or way of working and what they need to do to improve their security. This personal risk assessment is only a guide to where improvements could be made to your personal security. When a security improvement is made, it is generally referred to as a 'control' because it controls a risk or vulnerability.

There are many more controls, or improvements, that can be made to your security online, but in the table below there are four in each group. These four should provide you with a basic level of security, but the more you can say 'Yes', the more secure you are.

Table 6: Cyber security risk assessment

	Page reference	Control	Not needed	Yes	No
Device		Have all unused applications been removed from the device?			
		Have all unused services on the device been disabled, such as the webcam?			

	Page reference	Control	Not needed	Yes	No
		Are automatic updates configured?			
		Is encryption applied?			
Malware		Has an antivirus application been installed and configured?			
		Has a VPN been installed?			
		Has a spam filter been installed?			
		Has an ad blocker been configured?			
Profile		Do you regularly search your online profile?			
		Have you spoken to family and friends about what they post about you?			
		Do you consider security and think about how this information could be used before you post?			
		Have you created an Internet alert for your own name?			

	Page reference	Control	Not needed	Yes	No
Accounts		Do you have a unique password or passphrase for each account and are these regularly changed?			
		Have you checked the strength of your password? *https://howsecurei smypassword.net/*			
		Are parental controls set on accounts that may need them to protect the account user?			
		Have you checked to see if any of your online accounts may have been pwned?			
Culture		Do you check the identity of all callers?			
		Do you check attachments are valid and/or expected before you open them?			
		Do you check these with the sender before you			

	Page reference	Control	Not needed	Yes	No
		click links in emails?			
		Do you check sender addresses before acting on or responding to emails?			
SNS		Do you know all your friends on social networking sites?			
		Have you limited the distribution of your posts?			
		Have you restricted who can see your profile?			
		Do you regularly review these settings on all your social networking accounts?			
Internet		Do you use a safe browser?			
		Has a web filter been installed?			
		Has a spam filter been installed?			
		Do you use a safe search engine?			

	Page reference	Control	Not needed	Yes	No
IoT		Have you changed the manufacturer's password?			
		Do you regularly change the password?			
		Do you have an IoT firewall?			
		Have you made sure the IoT device has not created extra risks?			
Parental		Do you talk to your children about their activities on the Internet?			
		Do you talk to your children about your activities on the Internet?			
		Have you shared the family Internet security tasks with your children – do they search you?			
		Do you talk about good things on the Internet as much as you talk about			

	Page reference	Control	Not needed	Yes	No
		Internet risks with your children?			
Financial		Do you visually and physically check ATMs before you use them?			
		Do you protect your contactless cards from being attacked or mistakenly charged?			
		Do you protect your PIN when buying things in shops?			
		Do you use ATMs in banks more often than those on the street?			
Mobile		Do you use a VPN if you connect to a public wireless network?			
		Do you make sure that you do not go to a sensitive website at the same time you are on social networking sites?			

	Page reference	Control	Not needed	Yes	No
		Do you use a screen filter or make sure no one is reading your screen?			
		Do you lock your screen or close your screen down if you have to move away from your device?			
Travel		Do you avoid using public USB charging points?			
		Do you keep your mobile devices with you when travelling?			
		Do you only use your own USB devices?			
		Do you use a hotspot more than public wireless networks when travelling within Europe?			

ITG RESOURCES

IT Governance Ltd sources, creates and delivers products and services to meet the real-world, evolving IT governance needs of today's organisations, directors, managers and practitioners.

The ITG website (*www.itgovernance.co.uk*) is the international one-stop-shop for corporate and IT governance information, advice, guidance, books, tools, training and consultancy. On the website you will find the following pages related to the subject matter of this book:

www.itgovernance.co.uk/what-is-cybersecurity

www.itgovernance.co.uk/infosec.aspx

www.itgovernance.co.uk/iso27001.aspx.

Publishing Services

IT Governance Publishing (ITGP) is the world's leading IT-GRC publishing imprint that is wholly owned by IT Governance Ltd.

With books and tools covering all IT governance, risk and compliance frameworks, we are the publisher of choice for authors and distributors alike, producing unique and practical publications of the highest quality, in the latest formats available, which readers will find invaluable.

www.itgovernancepublishing.co.uk is the website dedicated to ITGP. Other titles published by ITGP that may be of interest include:

- EU GDPR: A Pocket Guide
  www.itgovernance.co.uk/shop/product/eu-gdpr-a-pocket-guide

- Information Security: A Practical Guide
  www.itgovernance.co.uk/shop/product/information-security-a-practical-guide-bridging-the-gap-between-it-and-management

- CyberWar, CyberTerror, CyberCrime and CyberActivism
  www.itgovernance.co.uk/shop/product/cyberwar-cyberterror-cybercrime-and-cyberactivism-second-edition

We also offer a range of toolkits that give comprehensive, customisable documents to help users create the specific documentation they need to properly implement a management system or standard. Written by experienced practitioners and based on the latest best practice, ITGP toolkits can save months of work for organisations working towards compliance with a given standard.

To see the full range of toolkits available please visit:

www.itgovernance.co.uk/shop/category/itgp-toolkits.

Books and tools published by IT Governance Publishing (ITGP) are available from all business booksellers and the following websites:

www.itgovernance.eu   *www.itgovernanceusa.com*

www.itgovernancesa.co.za www.itgovernance.asia

Training Services

IT Governance is an acknowledged leader in the world of ISO 27001 and information security management training. Our practical, hands-on approach is delivered by experienced practitioners, who focus on improving your knowledge, developing your skills, and awarding relevant, industry-recognised certifications. Our fully integrated and structured learning paths accommodate delegates with various levels of knowledge, and our courses can be delivered in a variety of formats to suit all delegates.

For more information about IT Governance's ISO 27001 Learning Pathway, please see: *www.itgovernance.co.uk/ iso27001-information-security-training.aspx.*

For information on any of our many other courses, including PCI DSS compliance, business continuity, IT governance, service management and professional certification courses, please see: *www.itgovernance.co.uk/training.aspx*.

Professional Services and Consultancy

ISO 27001, the international standard for information security management, sets out the requirements of an information security management system (ISMS), a holistic approach to information security that encompasses people, processes, and technology. Only by using this approach to information security can organisations hope to instil an enterprise-wide security culture.

Implementing, maintaining and continually improving an ISMS can, however, be a daunting task. Fortunately, IT Governance's consultants offer a comprehensive range of flexible, practical support packages to help organisations of any size, sector or location to implement an ISMS and achieve certification to ISO 27001.

For more information on our ISO 27001 consultancy service, please see:

www.itgovernance.co.uk/iso27001_consultancy.aspx.

For general information about our other consultancy services, including for ISO20000, ISO22301, Cyber Essentials, the PCI DSS, Data Protection and more, please see: *www.itgovernance.co.uk/consulting.aspx*

Newsletter

You can stay up to date with the latest developments across the whole spectrum of IT governance subject matter — including risk management, information security, ITIL and IT service management, project governance, compliance, and so much more — by subscribing to our newsletter.

Simply visit our subscription center and select your preferences: *www.itgovernance.co.uk/daily-sentinel*.

EU for product safety is Stephen Evans, The Mill Enterprise Hub, Stagreenan, Drogheda, Co. Louth, A92 CD3D, Ireland. (servicecentre@itgovernance.eu)